D.L. Nicholson

April '36

THE
PHOENIX LIBRARY

★

FIRST PLAYS

*A list
of other titles in the Phoenix Library
will be found at the end
of this book*

FIRST PLAYS

WURZEL-FLUMMERY : THE LUCKY ONE :
THE BOY COMES HOME : BELINDA :
THE RED FEATHERS

By

A. A. MILNE

CHATTO AND WINDUS
LONDON

TO
MY MOTHER

First published September 1919
First issued in the Phoenix Library 1928
reprinted 1929

CONTENTS

INTRODUCTION

THESE five plays were written, in the order in which they appear now, during the years 1916 and 1917. They would hardly have been written had it not been for the war, although only one of them is concerned with that subject. To his other responsibilities the Kaiser now adds this volume.

For these plays were not the work of a professional writer, but the recreation of a (temporary) professional soldier. Play-writing is a luxury to a journalist, as insidious as golf and much more expensive in time and money. When an article is written, the financial reward (and we may as well live as not) is a matter of certainty. A novelist, too, even if he is not in "the front rank"—but I never heard of one who wasn't—can at least be sure of publication. But when a play is written, there is no certainty of anything save disillusionment.

To write a play, then, while I was a journalist seemed to me a depraved proceeding, almost as bad as going to Lord's in the morning. I thought I could write one (we all think we can), but I could not afford so unpromising a gamble. But once in the Army the case was altered. No duty now urged me to write. My job was soldiering, and my spare time was my own affair. Other subalterns played bridge and golf; that was one way of amusing oneself. Another way was—why not?—to write plays.

So we began with *Wurzel-Flummery*. I say "we," because another is mixed up in this business even more seriously than the Kaiser. She wrote; I dictated. And if a particularly fine evening drew us out for a walk along the byways—where there was no saluting, and one could smoke a pipe without shocking the Duke of Cambridge—then it was to discuss the last scene and to wonder what would happen in the next. We did not estimate the money or publicity which might come from this new venture; there has never been any serious thought of making money by my bridge-playing, nor desire for publicity when I am trying to play golf. But secretly, of course, we hoped. It was that which made it so much more exciting than any other game.

Our hopes were realized to the following extent:

Wurzel-Flummery was produced by Mr. Dion Boucicault at the New Theatre in April, 1917. It was originally written in three acts, in which form it was shown to one or two managers. At the beginning of 1917 I was offered the chance of production in a triple bill if I cut it down into a two-act play. To cut even a line is painful, but to cut thirty pages of one's first comedy, slaughtering whole characters on the way, has at least a certain morbid fascination. It appeared, therefore, in two acts; and one kindly critic embarrassed us by saying that a lesser artist would have written it in three acts, and most of the other critics annoyed us by saying that a greater artist would have written it in one act. However, I amused myself some months later by slaying another character—the office-boy, no less—thereby getting it down to one act, and was surprised to find that the one-act version was, after all, the best. . . At least I think it is. . . . At any rate, that is the version I am printing here ; but, as can be imagined, I am rather tired of the whole business by now, and I am beginning to wonder if anyone ever did take the name of Wurzel-Flummery at all. Probably the whole thing is an invention.

The Lucky One was doomed from the start with a name like that. And the girl marries the wrong man. I see no hope of its being produced. But if any critic wishes to endear himself to me (though I don't see why he should) he will agree with me that it is the best play of the five.

The Boy Comes Home was produced by Mr. Owen Nares at the Victoria Palace in September, 1918, introduced afterwards into *Hallo, America !* at the Palace and played by Mr. Godfrey Tearle at the Coliseum in the following April.

Belinda was produced by Mr. Dion Boucicault at the New Theatre in April, 1918, with Miss Irene Vanbrugh in the name-part. Miss Ethel Barrymore played it in New York. I hope it will read pleasantly, but I am quite incapable of judging it, for every speech of Belinda's comes to me now in Miss Vanbrugh's voice.

The Red Feathers has not yet been produced, one reason being (perhaps) that it has never been offered to anybody.   It is difficult enough to find a manager, but when one has also to get hold of a composer, the business of production becomes terrifying.   I suppose there is a way of negotiating these difficulties, but I suspect that most of the fun to be got out of this operetta we have already had in writing it.

In conclusion, I must distress my friend J. M. Barrie (who gave me a first chance) by acknowledging my great debt to him.   It would be more polite to leave him out of it, but I cannot let him off.   After all, these are only " First Plays."   I can always hope that " Last Plays" will be more worthy of that early encouragement.

A. A. MILNE.

WURZEL-FLUMMERY

A COMEDY IN ONE ACT

CHARACTERS.

Robert Crawshaw, M.P.
Margaret Crawshaw (*his wife*).
Viola Crawshaw (*his daughter*).
Richard Meriton, M.P.
Denis Clifton.

A two-act version of this play was produced by Mr. Dion Boucicault at the New Theatre on April 7, 1917, with the following cast:

Robert Crawshaw -	-	Nigel Playfair.
Margaret Crawshaw	-	Helen Haye.
Viola Crawshaw -	-	Peggy Kurton.
Richard Meriton -	-	Martin Lewis.
Denis Clifton -	-	Dion Boucicault.
Lancelot Dodd -	-	Bertram Siems.

WURZEL-FLUMMERY

SCENE.—ROBERT CRAWSHAW'S *town house.   Morning.*

It is a June day before the war in the morning-room of
ROBERT CRAWSHAW'S *town house.   Entering it with our
friend the house-agent, our attention would first be
called to the* delightful club fender round the fireplace.
On one side of this *a Chesterfield sofa comes out at
right angles.   In a corner of the sofa* MISS VIOLA
CRAWSHAW *is sitting, deep in " The Times."   The
house-agent would hesitate to* catalogue her, *but we
notice for ourselves, before he points out the comfortable*
armchair opposite, *that she is young and pretty.   In
the middle of the room and facing the fireplace is
(*observe*) a solid knee-hole writing-table, covered with
papers and books of reference, and supported by a chair
at the middle and another at the side.   The rest of the
furniture, and the books and pictures round the walls,
we must leave until another time, for at this moment
the door behind the sofa opens and* RICHARD MERITON
*comes in.   He looks about thirty-five, has a clean-shaven
intelligent face, and is dressed in a dark tweed suit.
We withdraw hastily, as he comes behind* VIOLA *and
puts his hands over her eyes.*

RICHARD. Three guesses who it is.

VIOLA (*putting her hands over his*). The Archbishop of
Canterbury.

RICHARD. No.

VIOLA. The Archbishop of York.

3

RICHARD. Fortunately that exhausts the archbishops. Now, then, your last guess.

VIOLA. Richard Meriton, M.P.

RICHARD. Wonderful ! (*He kisses the top of her head lightly and goes round to the club fender, where he sits with his back to the fireplace.*) How did you know ? (*He begins to fill a pipe.*)

VIOLA (*smiling*). Well, it couldn't have been father.

RICHARD. N-no, I suppose not. Not just after breakfast anyway. Anything in the paper ?

VIOLA. There's a letter from father pointing out that——

RICHARD. I never knew such a man as Robert for pointing out.

VIOLA. Anyhow, it's in big print.

RICHARD. It would be.

VIOLA. You are very cynical this morning, Dick.

RICHARD. The sausages were cold, dear.

VIOLA. Poor Dick ! Oh, Dick, I wish you were on the same side as father.

RICHARD. But he's on the wrong side. Surely I've told you that before. . . . Viola, do you really think it would make a difference ?

VIOLA. Well, you know what he said about you at Basingstoke the other day.

RICHARD. No, I don't, really.

VIOLA. He said that your intellectual arrogance was only equalled by your spiritual instability. I don't quite know what it means, but it doesn't sound the sort of thing you want in a son-in-law.

RICHARD. Still, it was friendly of him to go right away to Basingstoke to say it. Anyhow, you don't believe it.

VIOLA. Of course not.

RICHARD. And Robert doesn't really.

VIOLA. Then why does he say it ?

RICHARD. Ah, now you're opening up very grave

questions. The whole structure of the British Constitution rests upon Robert's right to say things like that at Basingstoke. . . . But really, darling, we're very good friends. He's always asking my advice about things— he doesn't take it, of course, but still he asks it ; and it was awfully good of him to insist on my staying here while my flat was being done up. (*Seriously*) I bless him for that. If it hadn't been for the last week I should never have known you. You were just " Viola " —the girl I'd seen at odd times since she was a child ; and now—oh, why won't you let me tell your father ? I hate it like this.

VIOLA. Because I love you, Dick, and because I know father. He would, as they say in novels, show you the door. (*Smiling*) And I want you this side of the door for a little bit longer.

RICHARD (*firmly*). I shall tell him before I go.

VIOLA (*pleadingly*). But not till then ; that gives us two more days. You see, darling, it's going to take me all I know to get round him. You see, apart from politics you're so poor—and father hates poor people.

RICHARD (*viciously*). Damn money !

VIOLA (*thoughtfully*). I think that's what father means by spiritual instability.

RICHARD. Viola ! (*He stands up and holds out his arms to her. She goes to him and——*) Oh, Lord, look out !

VIOLA (*reaching across to the mantelpiece*). Matches ?

RICHARD. Thanks very much. (*He lights his pipe as* ROBERT CRAWSHAW *comes in.*)

> (CRAWSHAW *is forty-five, but his closely-trimmed moustache and whiskers, his inclination to stoutness, and the loud old-gentlemanly style in trousers which he affects with his morning-coat, make him look older, and, what is more important, the Pillar of the State which he undoubtedly is.*)

CRAWSHAW. Good-morning, Richard. Down at last?

RICHARD. Good-morning. I did warn you, didn't I, that I was bad at breakfasts?

CRAWSHAW. Viola, where's your mother?

VIOLA (*making for the door*). I don't know, father· do you want her?

CRAWSHAW. I wish to speak to her.

VIOLA. All right, I'll tell her.   [*She goes out.*

(RICHARD *picks up "The Times" and sits down again.*)

CRAWSHAW (*sitting down in a business-like way at his desk*). Richard, why don't you get something to do?

RICHARD. My dear fellow, I've only just finished break-fast.

SHAW. I mean generally. And apart, of course, from your—ah—work in the House.

RICHARD (*a trifle cool*). I have something to do.

CRAWSHAW. Oh, reviewing. I mean something serious. You should get a directorship or something in the City.

RICHARD. I hate the City.

CRAWSHAW. Ah! there, my dear Richard, is that intellectual arrogance to which I had to call attention the other day at Basingstoke.

RICHARD (*drily*). Yes, so Viola was telling me.

CRAWSHAW. You understood, my dear fellow, that I meant nothing personal. (*Clearing his throat*) It is justly one of the proudest boasts of the Englishman that his political enmities are not allowed to interfere with his private friendships.

RICHARD (*carelessly*). Oh, I shall go to Basingstoke myself one day.

Enter MARGARET. MARGARET *has been in love with* ROBERT
CRAWSHAW *for twenty-five years, the last twenty-four
years from habit. She is small, comfortable, and
rather foolish; you would certainly call her a dear, but
you might sometimes call her a poor dear.*

MARGARET. Good-morning, Mr. Meriton. I do hope
your breakfast was all right.

RICHARD. Excellent, thank you.

MARGARET. That's right. Did you want me, Robert?

CRAWSHAW (*obviously uncomfortable*). Yes—er—h'r'm
—Richard—er—what are your—er—plans?

RICHARD. Is he trying to get rid of me, Mrs
Crawshaw?

MARGARET. Of course not. (*To* ROBERT) Are you,
dear?

CRAWSHAW. Perhaps we had better come into my room,
Margaret. We can leave Richard here with the paper.

RICHARD. No, no; I'm going.

CRAWSHAW (*going to the door with him*). I have some
particular business to discuss. If you aren't going out,
I should like to consult you in the matter afterwards.

RICHARD. Right!   [*He goes out.*

CRAWSHAW. Sit down, Margaret. I have some extraordinary news for you.

MARGARET (*sitting down*). Yes, Robert?

CRAWSHAW. This letter has just come by hand. (*He
reads it*) "199, Lincoln's Inn Fields. Dear Sir, I have
the pleasure to inform you that under the will of the
late Mr. Antony Clifton you are a beneficiary to the
extent of £50,000."

MARGARET. Robert!

CRAWSHAW. Wait! "A trifling condition is attached—
namely, that you should take the name of—Wurzel-
Flummery."

MARGARET. Robert!

CRAWSHAW. "I have the honour to be, your obedient servant, Denis Clifton." (*He folds the letter up and puts it away.*)

MARGARET. Robert, whoever is he? I mean the one who's left you the money?

CRAWSHAW (*calmly*). I have not the slightest idea, Margaret. Doubtless we shall find out before long. I have asked Mr. Denis Clifton to come and see me.

MARGARET. Leaving you fifty thousand pounds! Just fancy!

CRAWSHAW. Wurzel-Flummery!

MARGARET. We can have the second car now, dear, can't we? And what about moving? You know you always said you ought to be in a more central part. Mr. Robert Crawshaw, M.P., of Curzon Street sounds so much more—more Cabinety.

CRAWSHAW. Mr. Robert Wurzel-Flummery, M.P., of Curzon Street—I don't know what *that* sounds like.

MARGARET. I expect that's only a legal way of putting it, dear. They can't really expect us to change our name to—Wurzley-Fothergill.

CRAWSHAW. Wurzel-Flummery.

MARGARET. Yes, dear, didn't I say that? I am sure you could talk the solicitor round—this Mr. Denis Clifton. After all, it doesn't matter to *him* what we call ourselves. Write him one of your letters, dear.

CRAWSHAW. You don't seem to apprehend the situation Margaret.

MARGARET. Yes, I do, dear. This Mr.—Mr.——

CRAWSHAW. Antony Clifton.

MARGARET. Yes, he's left you fifty thousand pounds, together with the name of Wurzley-Fothergill——

CRAWSHAW. Wurzel—oh, well, never mind.

MARGARET. Yes, well, you tell the solicitor that you

will take the fifty thousand pounds, but you don't want the name. It's too absurd, when everybody knows of Robert Crawshaw, M.P., to expect you to call yourself Wurzley-Fothergill.

CRAWSHAW (*impatiently*). Yes, yes. The point is that this Mr. Clifton has left me the money on *condition* that I change my name. If I don't take the name, I don't take the money.

MARGARET. But is that legal?

CRAWSHAW. Perfectly. It is often done. People change their names on succeeding to some property.

MARGARET. I thought it was only when your name was Moses and you changed it to Talbot.

CRAWSHAW (*to himself*). Wurzel-Flummery!

MARGARET. I wonder why he left you the money at all. Of course it was very nice of him, but if you didn't know him—— Why do you think he did, dear?

CRAWSHAW. I know no more than this letter. I suppose he had—ah—followed my career, and was—ah—interested in it, and being a man with no relations, felt that he could—ah—safely leave this money to me. No doubt Wurzel-Flummery was his mother's maiden name, or the name of some other friend even dearer to him; he wished the name—ah—perpetuated, perhaps even recorded not unworthily in the history of our country, and—ah—made this will accordingly. In a way it is a kind of—ah—sacred trust.

MARGARET. Then, of course, you'll accept it, dear?

CRAWSHAW. It requires some consideration. I have my career to think about, my duty to my country.

MARGARET. Of course, dear. Money is a great help in politics, isn't it?

CRAWSHAW. Money wisely spent is a help in any profession. The view of riches which socialists and suchlike people profess to take is entirely ill-considered.

A rich man, who spends his money thoughtfully, is serving his country as nobly as anybody.

MARGARET. Yes, dear. Then you think we *could* have that second car and the house in Curzon Street?

CRAWSHAW. We must not be led away. Fifty thousand pounds, properly invested, is only two thousand a year. When you have deducted the income-tax—and the tax on unearned income is extremely high just now——

MARGARET. Oh, but surely if we have to call ourselves Wurzel-Flummery it would count as *earned* income.

CRAWSHAW. I fear not. Strictly speaking, all money is earned. Even if it is left to you by another, it is presumably left to you in recognition of certain outstanding qualities which you possess. But Parliament takes a different view. I do not for a moment say that fifty thousand pounds would not be welcome. Fifty thousand pounds is certainly not to be sneezed at——

MARGARET. I should think not, indeed!

CRAWSHAW (*unconsciously rising from his chair*). And without this preposterous condition attached I should be pleased to accept this trust, and I would endeavour, Mr. Speaker—— (*He sits down again suddenly.*) I would endeavour, Margaret, to carry it out to the best of my poor ability. But—Wurzel-Flummery!

MARGARET. You would soon get used to it, dear. I had to get used to the name of Crawshaw after I had been Debenham for twenty-five years. It is surprising how quickly it comes to you. I think I only signed my name Margaret Debenham once after I was married.

CRAWSHAW (*kindly*). The cases are rather different, Margaret. Naturally a woman, who from her cradle looks forward to the day when she will change her name, cannot have this feeling for the—ah—honour of

his name, which every man—ah—feels.   Such a feeling
is naturally more present in my own case since I have
been privileged to make the name of Crawshaw in some
degree—ah—well-known, I might almost say famous.

MARGARET (*wistfully*). I used to be called "the
beautiful Miss Debenham of Leamington."   Everybody
in Leamington knew of me.   Of course, I am very proud
to be Mrs. Robert Crawshaw.

CRAWSHAW (*getting up and walking over to the fireplace*).
In a way it would mean beginning all over again.   It is
half the battle in politics to get your name before the
public.   "Whoever is this man Wurzel-Flummery?"
people will say.

MARGARET. Anyhow, dear, let us look on the bright
side.   Fifty thousand pounds is fifty thousand pounds.

CRAWSHAW. It is, Margaret.   And no doubt it is my
duty to accept it.   But—well, all I say is that a
gentleman would have left it without any conditions.
Or at least he would merely have expressed his *wish*
that I should take the name, without going so far as to
enforce it.   Then I could have looked at the matter all
round in an impartial spirit.

MARGARET (*pursuing her thoughts*). The linen is
marked R. M. C. now.   Of course, we should have to
have that altered.   Do you think R. M. F. would do,
or would it have to be R. M. W. hyphen F.?

CRAWSHAW. What?   Oh—yes, there will be a good
deal of that to attend to.   (*Going up to her*) I think,
Margaret, I had better talk to Richard about this.   Of
course, it would be absurd to refuse the money, but—
well, I should like to have his opinion.

MARGARET (*getting up*). Do you think he would be
very sympathetic, dear?   He makes jokes about serious
things—like bishops and hunting—just as if they
weren't at all serious.

CRAWSHAW. I wish to talk to him just to obtain a new
—ah—point of view. I do not hold myself in the least
bound to act on anything he says. I regard him as a
constituent, Margaret.

MARGARET. Then I will send him to you.

CRAWSHAW (*putting his hands on her shoulders*). Margaret, what do you really feel about it ?

MARGARET. Just whatever *you* feel, Robert.

CRAWSHAW (*kissing her*). Thank you, Margaret; you
are a good wife to me.   [*She goes out*

> (CRAWSHAW *goes to his desk and selects a " Who's
> Who " from a little pile of reference-books on
> it. He walks round to his chair, sits down in
> it and begins to turn the pages, murmuring
> names beginning with " C " to himself as he
> gets near the place. When he finds it, he
> murmurs " Clifton—that's funny," and closes
> the book. Evidently the publishers have failed
> him.*)

Enter RICHARD.

RICHARD. Well, what's the news ?   (*He goes to his
old seat on the fender.*)   Been left a fortune ?

CRAWSHAW (*simply*). Yes. . . .   By a Mr. Antony
Clifton.   I never met him and I know nothing about him.

RICHARD (*surprised*). Not really ?   Well, I congratulate you.   (*He sighs.*)   To them that hath—— But
what on earth do you want my advice about ?

CRAWSHAW. There is a slight condition attached.

RICHARD. Oho !

CRAWSHAW. The condition is that with this money—
fifty thousand pounds—I take the name of—ah—
Wurzel-Flummery.

RICHARD (*jumping up*). What !

CRAWSHAW (*sulkily*). I said it quite distinctly — Wurzel-Flummery.

> (RICHARD *in an awed silence walks over to the desk and stands looking down at the unhappy* CRAWSHAW. *He throws out his left hand as if introducing him.*)

RICHARD (*reverently*). Mr. Robert Wurzel-Flummery, M.P., one of the most prominent of our younger Parliamentarians. Oh, you . . . oh ! . . . oh, how too heavenly ! (*He goes back to his seat, looks up and catches* CRAWSHAW'S *eye, and breaks down altogether.*)

CRAWSHAW (*rising with dignity*). Shall we discuss it seriously, or shall we leave it ?

RICHARD. How can we discuss a name like Wurzel-Flummery seriously ? "Mr. Wurzel-Flummery in a few well-chosen words seconded the motion." . . . "'Sir,' went on Mr. Wurzel-Flummery "—— Oh, poor Robert !

CRAWSHAW (*sitting down sulkily*). You seem quite certain that I shall take the money.

RICHARD. I am quite certain.

CRAWSHAW. Would *you* take it ?

RICHARD (*hesitating*). Well—I wonder.

CRAWSHAW. After all, as William Shakespeare says, "What's in a name ?"

RICHARD. I can tell you something else that Shakespeare — *William* Shakespeare — said. (*Dramatically rising*) Who steals my purse with fifty thousand in it—steals trash. (*In his natural voice*) Trash, Robert: (*Dramatically again*) But he who filches from me my good name of Crawshaw (*lightly*) and substitutes the rotten one of Wurzel——

CRAWSHAW (*annoyed*). As a matter of fact, Wurzel-Flummery is a very good old name. I seem to remember some—ah—Hampshire Wurzel-Flummeries.

It is a very laudable spirit on the part of a dying man to wish to—ah—perpetuate these old English names. It all seems to me quite natural and straightforward. If I take this money I shall have nothing to be ashamed of.

RICHARD. I see. . . . Look here, may I ask you a few questions? I should like to know just how you feel about the whole business?

CRAWSHAW (*complacently folding his hands*). Go ahead.

RICHARD. Suppose a stranger came up in the street to you and said, "My poor man, here's five pounds for you," what would you do? Tell him to go to the devil, I suppose, wouldn't you?

CRAWSHAW (*humorously*). In more parliamentary language, perhaps, Richard. I should tell him I never took money from strangers.

RICHARD. Quite so; but that if it were ten thousand pounds, you would take it?

CRAWSHAW. I most certainly shouldn't.

RICHARD. But if he died and left it to you, *then* you would?

CRAWSHAW (*blandly*). Ah, I thought you were leading up to that. That, of course, is entirely different.

RICHARD. Why?

CRAWSHAW. Well—ah—wouldn't *you* take ten thousand pounds if it were left to you by a stranger?

RICHARD. I daresay I should. But I should like to know why it would seem different.

CRAWSHAW (*professionally*). Ha—hum! Well—in the first place, when a man is dead he wants his money no longer. You can therefore be certain that you are not taking anything from him which he cannot spare. And in the next place, it is the man's dying wish that you should have the money. To refuse would be to refuse the dead. To accept becomes almost a sacred duty.

RICHARD. It really comes to this, doesn't it? You won't take it from him when he's alive, because if you did, you couldn't decently refuse him a little gratitude; but you know that it doesn't matter a damn to him what happens to his money after he's dead, and therefore you can take it without feeling any gratitude at all.

CRAWSHAW. No, I shouldn't put it like that.

RICHARD (*smiling*). I'm sure you wouldn't, Robert.

CRAWSHAW. No doubt you can twist it about so that——

RICHARD. All right, we'll leave that and go on to the next point. Suppose a perfect stranger offered you five pounds to part your hair down the middle, shave off your moustache, and wear only one whisker—if he met you suddenly in the street, seemed to dislike your appearance, took out a fiver and begged you to hurry off and alter yourself—of course you'd pocket the money and go straight to your barber's?

CRAWSHAW. Now you are merely being offensive.

RICHARD. I beg your pardon. I should have said that if he had left you five pounds in his will?—well, then twenty pounds?—a hundred pounds?—a thousand pounds?—fifty thousand pounds?—— (*Jumping up excitedly*) It's only a question of price—fifty thousand pounds, Robert—a pink tie with purple spots, hair parted across the back, trousers with a patch in the seat, call myself Wurzel-Flummery—any old thing you like, you can't insult me—anything you like, gentlemen, for fifty thousand pounds. (*Lowering his voice*) Only you must leave it in your will, and then I can feel that it is a sacred duty—a sacred duty, my lords and gentlemen. (*He sinks back into the sofa and relights his pipe.*)

CRAWSHAW. (*rising with dignity*). It is evidently useless to prolong this conversation.

RICHARD (*waving him down again*). No, no, Robert; I've finished. I just took the other side—and I got carried away. I ought to have been at the Bar.

CRAWSHAW. You take such extraordinary views of things. You must look facts in the face, Richard. This is a modern world, and we are modern people living in it. Take the matter-of-fact view. You may like or dislike the name of—ah—Wurzel-Flummery, but you can't get away from the fact that fifty thousand pounds is not to be sneezed at.

RICHARD (*wistfully*). I don't know why people shouldn't sneeze at money sometimes. I should like to start a society for sneezing at fifty thousand pounds. We'd have to begin in a small way, of course ; we'd begin by sneezing at five pounds—and work up. . . . The trouble is that we're all inoculated in our cradles against that kind of cold.

CRAWSHAW (*pleasantly*). You will have your little joke. But you know as well as I do that it is only a joke. There can be no serious reason why I should not take this money. And I—ah—gather that you don't think it will affect my career?

RICHARD (*carelessly*). Not a bit. It'll help it. It'll get you into all the comic papers.

MARGARET *comes in at this moment, to the relief of* CRAW-SHAW, *who is not quite certain if he is being flattered or insulted again.*

MARGARET. Well, have you told him?

RICHARD (*making way for her on the sofa*). I have heard the news, Mrs. Crawshaw. And I have told Robert my opinion that he should have no difficulty in making the name of Wurzel-Flummery as famous as he has already made that of Crawshaw. At any rate I hope he will.

MARGARET. How nice of you!

CRAWSHAW. Well, it's settled, then. (*Looking at his watch*) This solicitor fellow should be here soon. Perhaps, after all, we can manage something about—— Ah, Viola, did you want your mother?

Enter VIOLA.

VIOLA. Sorry, do I interrupt a family meeting? There's Richard, so it can't be very serious.

RICHARD. What a reputation!

CRAWSHAW. Well, it's over now.

MARGARET. Viola had better know, hadn't she?

CRAWSHAW. She'll have to know some time, of course.

VIOLA (*sitting down firmly on the sofa*). Of course she will. So you'd better tell her now. I knew there was something exciting going on this morning.

CRAWSHAW (*embarrassed*). Hum—ha—— (*To* MARGARET) Perhaps you'd better tell her, dear.

MARGARET (*simply and naturally*). Father has come into some property, Viola. It means changing our name unfortunately. But your father doesn't think it will matter.

VIOLA. How thrilling! What is the name, mother?

MARGARET. Your father says it is—dear me, I shall never remember it.

CRAWSHAW (*mumbling*). Wurzel-Flummery.

VIOLA (*after a pause*). Dick, *you* tell me, if nobody else will.

RICHARD. Robert said it just now.

VIOLA. That wasn't a name, was it? I thought it was just a—do say it again, father.

CRAWSHAW (*sulkily but plainly*). Wurzel-Flummery.

VIOLA (*surprised*). Do you spell it like that? I mean like a wurzel and like flummery?

RICHARD. Exactly, I believe.

VIOLA (*to herself*). Miss Viola Wurzel-Flummery—I mean they'd have to look at you, wouldn't they? (*Bubbling over*) Oh, Dick, what a heavenly name! Who had it first?

RICHARD. They are an old Hampshire family—that is so, isn't it, Robert?

CRAWSHAW (*annoyed*). I said I thought that I remembered—Margaret, can you find Burke there?

(*She finds it, and he buries himself in the families of the great.*)

MARGARET. Well, Viola, you haven't told us how you like being Miss Wurzel-Flummery.

VIOLA. I haven't realized myself yet, mummy. I shall have to stand in front of my glass and tell myself who I am.

RICHARD. It's all right for *you*. You know you'll change your name one day, and then it won't matter what you've been called before.

VIOLA (*secretly*). H'sh! (*She smiles lovingly at him, and then says aloud*) Oh, won't it? It's got to appear in the papers, " A marriage has been arranged between Miss Viola Wurzel-Flummery . . ." and everybody will say, " And about time too, poor girl."

MARGARET (*to* CRAWSHAW). Have you found it, dear?

CRAWSHAW (*resentfully*). This is the 1912 edition.

MARGARET. Still, dear, if it's a very old family, it ought to be in by then.

VIOLA. I don't mind how old it is ; I think it's lovely. Oh, Dick, what fun it will be being announced! Just think of the footman throwing open the door and saying——

MAID (*announcing*). Mr. Denis Clifton.

(*There is a little natural confusion as* CLIFTON *enters jauntily in his summer suiting with a bundle of papers under his arm.* CRAWSHAW *goes towards him and shakes hands.*)

CRAWSHAW. How do you do, Mr. Clifton? Very good of you to come. (*Looking doubtfully at his clothes*) Er— it is Mr. Denis Clifton, the solicitor?

CLIFTON (*cheerfully*). It is. I must apologize for not looking the part more, but my clothes did not arrive from Clarkson's in time. Very careless of them when they had promised. And my clerk dissuaded me from the side-whiskers which I keep by me for these occasions.

CRAWSHAW (*bewildered*). Ah yes, quite so. But you have—ah—full legal authority to act in this matter?

CLIFTON. Oh, decidedly. Oh, there's no question of that.

CRAWSHAW (*introducing*). My wife — and daughter. (CLIFTON *bows gracefully.*) My friend, Mr. Richard Meriton.

CLIFTON (*happily*). Dear me! Mr. Meriton too! This is quite a situation, as we say in the profession.

RICHARD (*amused by him*). In the legal profession?

CLIFTON. In the theatrical profession. (*Turning to* MARGARET) I am a writer of plays, Mrs. Crawshaw. I am not giving away a professional secret when I tell you that most of the managers in London have thanked me for submitting my work to them.

CRAWSHAW (*firmly*). I understood, Mr. Clifton, that you were the solicitor employed to wind up the affairs of the late Mr. Antony Clifton.

CLIFTON. Oh, certainly. Oh, there's no doubt about my being a solicitor. My clerk, a man of the utmost integrity, not to say probity, would give me a reference. I am in the books; I belong to the Law Society. But my heart turns elsewhere. Officially I have embraced the profession of a solicitor—— (*Frankly, to* MRS. CRAWSHAW) But you know what these official embraces are.

MARGARET. I'm afraid—— (*She turns to her husband for assistance.*)

CLIFTON (*to* RICHARD). Unofficially, Mr. Meriton, I am wedded to the Muses.

VIOLA. Dick, isn't he lovely ?

CRAWSHAW. Quite so. But just for the moment, Mr. Clifton, I take it that we are concerned with legal business. Should I ever wish to produce a play, the case would be different.

CLIFTON. Admirably put. Pray regard me entirely as the solicitor for as long as you wish. (*He puts his hat down on a chair with the papers in it, and taking off his gloves, goes on dreamily*) Mr. Denis Clifton was superb as a solicitor. In spite of an indifferent make-up, his manner of taking off his gloves and dropping them into his hat—— (*He does so.*)

MARGARET (*to* CRAWSHAW). I think, perhaps, Viola and I——

RICHARD (*making a move too*). We'll leave you to your business, Robert.

CLIFTON (*holding up his hand*). Just one moment if I may. I have a letter for you, Mr. Meriton.

RICHARD (*surprised*). For me ?

CLIFTON. Yes. My clerk, a man of the utmost integrity—oh, but I said that before—he took it round to your rooms this morning, but found only painters and decorators there. (*He is feeling in his pockets and now brings the letter out.*) I brought it along, hoping that Mr. Crawshaw—but of course I never expected anything so delightful as this. (*He hands over the letter with a bow.*)

RICHARD. Thanks. (*He puts it in his pocket.*)

CLIFTON. Oh, but do read it now, won't you ? (*To* MRS. CRAWSHAW) One so rarely has an opportunity of being present when one's own letters are read. I think the habit they have on the stage of reading letters aloud to each other is such a very delightful one.

(RICHARD, *with a smile and a shrug, has opened his letter while* CLIFTON *is talking.*)

RICHARD. Good Lord !

VIOLA. Dick, what is it ?

RICHARD (*reading*). " 199, Lincoln's Inn Fields. Dear Sir, I have the pleasure to inform you that under the will of the late Mr. Antony Clifton you are a beneficiary to the extent of £50,000."

VIOLA. Dick !

RICHARD. " A trifling condition is attached—namely, that you should take the name of—Wurzel-Flummery."

(CLIFTON, *with his hand on his heart, bows gracefully from one to the other of them.*)

CRAWSHAW (*annoyed*). Impossible ! Why should he leave any money to *you ?*

VIOLA. Dick ! How wonderful !

MARGARET (*mildly*). I don't remember ever having had a morning quite like this.

RICHARD (*angrily*). Is this a joke, Mr. Clifton ?

CLIFTON. Oh, the money is there all right. My clerk, a man of the utmost——

RICHARD. Then I refuse it. I'll have nothing to do with it. I won't even argue about it. (*Tearing the letter into bits*) That's what I think of your money.

[*He stalks indignantly from the room.* EXIT

VIOLA. Dick ! Oh, but, mother, he mustn't. Oh, I must tell him—— [*She hurries after him.*

MARGARET (*with dignity*). Really, Mr. Clifton, I'm surprised at you. [*She goes out too*

CLIFTON (*looking round the room*). And now, Mr Crawshaw, we are alone.

CRAWSHAW. Yes. Well, I think, Mr. Clifton, you have a good deal to explain——

CLIFTON. My dear sir, I'm longing to begin. I have been looking forward to this day for weeks. I spent over an hour this morning dressing for it. (*He takes papers from his hat and moves to the sofa.*) Perhaps I had better begin from the beginning.

CRAWSHAW (*interested, indicating the papers*). The documents in the case?

CLIFTON. Oh dear, no—just something to carry in the hand. It makes one look more like a solicitor. (*Reading the title*) "Watherston v. Towser—*in re* Great Missenden Canal Company." My clerk invents the titles; it keeps him busy. He is very fond of Towser; Towser is always coming in. (*Frankly*) You see, Mr. Crawshaw, this is my first real case, and I only got it because Antony Clifton is my uncle. My efforts to introduce a little picturesqueness into the dull formalities of the law do not meet with that response that one would have expected.

CRAWSHAW (*looking at his watch*). Yes. Well, I'm a busy man, and if you could tell me as shortly as possible why your uncle left this money to me, and apparently to Mr. Meriton too, under these extraordinary conditions, I shall be obliged to you.

CLIFTON. Say no more, Mr. Crawshaw; I look forward to being entirely frank with you. It will be a pleasure.

CRAWSHAW. You understand, of course, my position. I think I may say that I am not without reputation in the country; and proud as I am to accept this sacred trust, this money which the late Mr. Antony Clifton has seen fit—(*modestly*) one cannot say why—to bequeath to me, yet the use of the name Wurzel-Flummery would be excessively awkward.

CLIFTON (*cheerfully*). Excessively.

CRAWSHAW. My object in seeing you was to inquire if

it was absolutely essential that the name should go
with the money.

CLIFTON. Well (*thoughtfully*), you may have the name
without the money if you like.   But you must have the
name.

CRAWSHAW (*disappointed*). Ah !   (*Bravely*) Of course,
I have nothing against the name, a good old Hampshire name——

CLIFTON (*shocked*). My dear Mr. Crawshaw, you didn't
think—you didn't really think that anybody had been
called Wurzel-Flummery before ?   Oh no, no.   You
and Mr. Meriton were to be the first, the founders of
the clan, the designers of the Wurzel-Flummery
sporran——

CRAWSHAW. What do you mean, sir ?   Are you telling
me that it is not a real name at all ?

CLIFTON. Oh, it's a name all right.   I know it is
because—er—*I* made it up.

CRAWSHAW (*outraged*). And you have the impu-
dence to propose, sir, that I should take a made-up
name ?

CLIFTON (*soothingly*). Well, all names are made up
some time or other.   Somebody had to think of—
Adam.

CRAWSHAW. I warn you, Mr. Clifton, that I do not
allow this trifling with serious subjects.

CLIFTON. It's all so simple, really. . . .   You see, my
Uncle Antony was a rather unusual man.   He despised
money.   He was not afraid to put it in its proper place.
The place he put it in was—er—a little below golf and
a little above classical concerts.   If a man said to him,
" Would you like to make fifty thousand this afternoon ?"
he would say—well, it would depend what he was
doing.   If he were going to have a round at Walton
Heath——

3

CRAWSHAW. It's perfectly scandalous to talk of money in this way.

CLIFTON. Well, that's how he talked about it. But he didn't find many to agree with him. In fact, he used to say that there was nothing, however contemptible, that a man would not do for money. One day I suggested that if he left a legacy with a sufficiently foolish name attached to it, somebody might be found to refuse it. He laughed at the idea. That put me on my mettle. "Two people," I said; "leave the same silly name to two people, two well-known people, rival politicians, say, men whose own names are already public property. Surely they wouldn't both take it." That touched him. "Denis, my boy, you've got it," he said. "Upon what vile bodies shall we experiment?" We decided on you and Mr. Meriton. The next thing was to choose the name. I started on the wrong lines. I began by suggesting names like Porker, Tosh, Bugge, Spiffkins—the obvious sort. My uncle——

CRAWSHAW (boiling with indignation). How dare you discuss me with your uncle, sir! How dare you decide in this cold-blooded way whether I am to be called—ah —Tosh—or—ah—Porker!

CLIFTON. My uncle wouldn't hear of Tosh or Porker. He wanted a humorous name—a name he could roll lovingly round his tongue—a name expressing a sort of humorous contempt—Wurzel-Flummery! I can see now the happy ruminating smile which came so often on my Uncle Antony's face in those latter months. He was thinking of his two Wurzel-Flummerys. I remember him saying once—it was at the Zoo—what a pity it was he hadn't enough to divide among the whole Cabinet. A whole bunch of Wurzel-Flummerys; it would have been rather jolly.

CRAWSHAW. You force me to say, sir, that if that was

the way you and your uncle used to talk together at the Zoo, his death can only be described as a merciful intervention of Providence.

CLIFTON. Oh, but I think he must be enjoying all this somewhere, you know. I hope he is. He would have loved this morning. It was his one regret that from the necessities of the case he could not live to enjoy his own joke ; but he had hopes that echoes of it would reach him wherever he might be. It was with some such idea, I fancy, that toward the end he became interested in spiritualism.

CRAWSHAW (*rising solemnly*). Mr. Clifton, I have no interest in the present whereabouts of your uncle, nor in what means he has of overhearing a private conversation between you and myself. But if, as you irreverently suggest, he is listening to us, I should like him to hear this. That, in my opinion, you are not a qualified solicitor at all, that you never had an uncle, and that the whole story of the will and the ridiculous condition attached to it is just the tomfool joke of a man who, by his own admission, wastes most of his time writing unsuccessful farces. And I propose——

CLIFTON. Pardon my interrupting. But you said farces. Not farces, comedies—of a whimsical nature.

CRAWSHAW. Whatever they were, sir, I propose to report the whole matter to the Law Society. And you know your way out, sir.

CLIFTON. Then I am to understand that you refuse the legacy, Mr. Crawshaw ?

CRAWSHAW (*startled*). What's that ?

CLIFTON. I am to understand that you refuse the fifty thousand pounds ?

CRAWSHAW. If the money is really there, I most certainly do not refuse it.

CLIFTON. Oh, the money is most certainly there—and the name. Both waiting for you.

CRAWSHAW (*thumping the table*). Then, sir, I accept them. I feel it my duty to accept them, as a public expression of confidence in the late Mr. Clifton's motives. I repudiate entirely the motives that you have suggested to him, and I consider it a sacred duty to show what I think of your story by accepting the trust which he has bequeathed to me. You will arrange further matters with my solicitor. Good-morning, sir.

CLIFTON (*to himself as he rises*). Mr. Crawshaw here drank a glass of water. (*To* CRAWSHAW) Mr. Wurzel-Flummery, farewell. May I express the parting wish that your future career will add fresh lustre to—my name: (*To himself as he goes out*) Exit Mr. Denis Clifton with dignity. (*But he has left his papers behind him.*)

 (CRAWSHAW, *walking indignantly back to the sofa, sees the papers and picks them up.*)

CRAWSHAW (*contemptuously*). "Watherston v. Towser—*in re* Great Missenden Canal Company." Bah! (*He tears them up and throws them into the fire. He goes back to his writing-table and is seated there as* VIOLA, *followed by* MERITON, *comes in.*)

ENTER

VIOLA. Father, Dick doesn't want to take the money, but I have told him that of course he must. He must, mustn't he?

RICHARD. We needn't drag Robert into it, Viola.

CRAWSHAW. If Richard has the very natural feeling that it would be awkward for me if there were two Wurzel-Flummerys in the House of Commons, I should be the last to interfere with his decision. In any case, I don't see what concern it is of yours, Viola.

VIOLA (*surprised*). But how can we get married if he doesn't take the money?

CRAWSHAW (*hardly understanding*). Married? What does this mean, Richard?

RICHARD. I'm sorry it has come out like this. We ought to have told you before, but anyhow we were going to have told you in a day or two. Viola and I want to get married.

CRAWSHAW. And what did you want to get married on?

RICHARD (*with a smile*). Not very much, I'm afraid.

VIOLA. We're all right now, father, because we shall have fifty thousand pounds.

RICHARD (*sadly*). Oh, Viola, Viola!

CRAWSHAW. But naturally this puts a very different complexion on matters.

VIOLA. So of course he must take it, mustn't he, father?

CRAWSHAW. I can hardly suppose, Richard, that you expect me to entrust my daughter to a man who is so little provident for himself that he throws away fifty thousand pounds because of some fanciful objection to the name which goes with it.

RICHARD (*in despair*). You don't understand, Robert.

CRAWSHAW. I understand this, Richard. That if the name is good enough for me, it should be good enough for you. You don't mind asking Viola to take *your* name, but you consider it an insult if you are asked to take *my* name.

RICHARD (*miserably to* VIOLA). Do you want to be Mrs. Wurzel-Flummery?

VIOLA. Well, I'm going to be Miss Wurzel-Flummery anyhow, darling.

RICHARD (*beaten*). Heaven help me! you'll make me take it. But you'll never understand.

CRAWSHAW (*stopping to administer comfort to him on his way out*). Come, come, Richard. (*Patting him on the shoulder*) I understand perfectly. All that you were saying about money a little while ago—it's all perfectly true, it's all just what I feel myself. But in practice we have to make allowances sometimes. We have to sacrifice our ideals for—ah—others. I shall be very proud to have you for a son-in-law, and to feel that there will be the two of us in Parliament together upholding the honour of the—ah—name. And perhaps now that we are to be so closely related, you may come to feel some day that your views could be—ah—more adequately put forward from *my* side of the House.

RICHARD. Go on, Robert; I deserve it.

CRAWSHAW. Well, well! Margaret will be interested in our news. And you must send that solicitor a line— or perhaps a telephone message would be better. (*He goes to the door and turns round just as he is going out.*) Yes, I think the telephone, Richard; it would be safer. [*Exit.*

RICHARD (*holding out his hands to* VIOLA). Come here, Mrs. Wurzel-Flummery.

VIOLA. Not Mrs. Wurzel-Flummery; Mrs. Dick. And soon, please, darling. (*She comes to him.*)

RICHARD (*shaking his head sadly at her*). I don't know what I've done, Viola. (*Suddenly*) But you're worth it. (*He kisses her, and then says in a low voice*) And God help me if I ever stop thinking so!

Enter MR. DENIS CLIFTON. *He sees them, and walks about very tactfully with his back towards them, humming to himself.*

RICHARD. Hullo!

CLIFTON (*to himself*). Now where did I put those papers? (*He hums to himself again.*) Now where—oh, I beg your pardon! I left some papers behind.

VIOLA. Dick, you'll tell him. (*As she goes out, she says to* CLIFTON) Good-bye, Mr. Clifton, and thank you for writing such nice letters.

CLIFTON. Good-bye, Miss Crawshaw.

VIOLA. Just say it to see how it sounds.

CLIFTON. Good-bye, Miss Wurzel-Flummery.

VIOLA (*smiling happily*). No, not Miss, *Mrs.*

[*She goes out.*

CLIFTON (*looking in surprise from her to him*). You don't mean——

RICHARD. Yes ; and I'm taking the money after all, Mr. Clifton.

CLIFTON. Dear me, what a situation ! (*Thoughtfully to himself*) I wonder how a rough scenario would strike the managers.

RICHARD. Poor Mr. Clifton !

CLIFTON. Why poor ?

RICHARD. You missed all the best part. You didn't hear what I said to Crawshaw about money before you came.

CLIFTON (*thoughtfully*). Oh ! was it very—— (*Brightening up*) But I expect Uncle Antony heard. (*After a pause*) Well, I must be getting on. I wonder if you've noticed any important papers lying about, in connection with the Great Missenden Canal Company— a most intricate case, in which my clerk and I—— (*He has murmured himself across to the fireplace, and the fragments of his important case suddenly catch his eye. He picks up one of the fragments.*) Ah, yes. Well, I shall tell my clerk that we lost the case. He will be sorry. He had got quite fond of that canal. (*He turns to go, but first says to* MERITON) So you're taking the money, Mr. Meriton ?

RICHARD. Yes.

CLIFTON. And Mr. Crawshaw too ?

RICHARD. Yes.

CLIFTON (*to himself as he goes out*). They are both taking it. (*He stops and looks up to* UNCLE ANTONY *with a smile.*) Good old Uncle Antony—*he* knew—*he* knew !

(MERITON *stands watching him as he goes.*)

THE LUCKY ONE

A PLAY IN THREE ACTS

CHARACTERS.

GERALD FARRINGDON.
BOB FARRINGDON (*his elder brother*).
SIR JAMES FARRINGDON (*his father*).
LADY FARRINGDON (*his mother*).
MISS FARRINGDON (*his great-aunt*).
PAMELA CAREY (*his betrothed*).
HENRY WENTWORTH ⎫
THOMAS TODD ⎬ (*his friends*).
LETTY HERBERT ⎭
MASON (*his old nurse*).

ACT I.

At SIR JAMES FARRINGDON'S *in the country.*

ACT II.

A private hotel in Dover Street. Two months later.

ACT III.

At SIR JAMES FARRINGDON'S *again. Three months later.*

THE LUCKY ONE

ACT I

SCENE.—*The hall of* SIR JAMES FARRINGDON'S *house in the country.*

It is a large and pleasantly unofficial sort of room, used as a meeting-place rather than a resting-place. To be in it pledges you to nothing ; whereas in the billiard-room you are presumably pledged to billiards. The French windows at the back open on to lawns ; the door on the right at the back will take you into the outer hall ; the door on the left leads to the servants' quarters ; the door on the right in front will disclose other inhabited rooms to you. An oak gallery runs round two sides of the hall and descends in broad and gentle stairs down the right side of it. Four stairs from the bottom it turns round at right angles and deposits you fairly in the hall. Entering in this way, you will see immediately opposite to you the large open fireplace occupied by a pile of unlit logs—for it is summer. There is a chair on each side of the fireplace, but turned now away from it. In the left centre of the hall there is a gate-legged table to which trays with drinks on them have a habit of finding their way ; it is supported on each side by a coffin-stool. A sofa, which will take two strangers comfortably and three friends less comfortably, comes out at right angles to the staircase,

*but leaves plenty of space between itself and the stool
on its side of the table.   Beneath the window on the
left of the French windows is a small table on which
letters and papers are put ; beneath the window on the
other side is a writing-table.   The walls are decorated
impartially with heads of wild animals and of Farringdons.*

At the present moment the inhabitants of the hall are three.
HENRY WENTWORTH, *a barrister between forty and
fifty, dressed in rather a serious tweed suit for a
summer day, is on the sofa.*   THOMAS TODD, *an
immaculate young gentleman of twenty-five, is half-
sitting on the gate-legged table with one foot on the
ground and the other swinging.   He is dressed in a
brown flannel coat and white trousers, shoes and socks,
and he has a putter in his hand indicative of his usual
line of thought.   The third occupant is the Butler, who, in
answer to* TOMMY's *ring, has appeared with the drinks.*
The time is about four o'clock on a June afternoon.

TOMMY (*to the Butler*). Thanks, James ; just leave it
here.   [*Exit Butler.*
Whisky or lemonade, Wentworth ?

WENTWORTH. Neither, thanks, Tommy.

TOMMY. Well, I will. (*He pours himself out some
lemonade and takes a long drink.*) I should have thought
you would have been thirsty, driving down from London
a day like this. (*He finishes his drink.*) Let's see,
where was I up to ? The sixth, wasn't it ?

WENTWORTH. The sixth, Tommy. (*With resignation*)
Only twelve more.

TOMMY. Yes, that's right. Well, at the seventh I got
an absolutely topping drive, but my approach was
sliced a bit. However, I chipped on within about six
feet, and was down in four   Gerald took it in three,

but I had a stroke, so I halved. Then the eighth I told you about.

WENTWORTH. Was that where you fell into the pond?

TOMMY. No, no; you're thinking of the fifth, where I topped my drive into the pond.

WENTWORTH. I knew the pond came into it somewhere. I hoped—I mean I thought you fell in.

TOMMY. Look here, you *must* remember the eighth, old chap; that was the one I did in one. Awful bit of luck.

WENTWORTH. Bit of luck for me too, Tommy.

TOMMY. Why?

WENTWORTH. Because now you can hurry on to the ninth.

TOMMY. I say, Wentworth, I thought you were keen on golf.

WENTWORTH. Only on my own.

TOMMY. You're a fraud. Here I've been absolutely wasting my precious time on you and—I suppose it wouldn't even interest you to hear that Gerald went round in seventy-two—five under bogey?

WENTWORTH. It would interest me much more to hear something about this girl he's engaged to.

TOMMY. Pamela Carey? Oh, she's an absolute ripper.

WENTWORTH. Yes, but you've said that of every girl you've met.

TOMMY. Well, dash it! you don't expect me to describe what she looks like, do you?

WENTWORTH. Well, no. I shall see that for myself directly. One gets introduced, you know, Tommy. It isn't as though I were meeting her at Charing Cross Station for the first time. But who is she?

TOMMY. Well, she was poor old Bob's friend originally.

He brought her down here, but, of course, as soon as she saw Gerald——

WENTWORTH (*quickly*). Why, *poor* old Bob?

TOMMY. I don't know; everybody seems to call him that. After all, he isn't quite like Gerald, is he?

WENTWORTH. Paderewski isn't quite like Tommy Todd, but I don't say " poor old Paderewski "—nor " poor old Tommy," if it comes to that.

TOMMY. Well, hang it, old man, there's a bit of a difference. Paderewski and I—well, I mean we don't compete.

WENTWORTH. Oh, I don't know. I daresay he's as rotten at golf as you, if the truth were really known.

TOMMY. No, but seriously, it's a bit different when you get two brothers like Gerald and Bob; and whatever the elder one does, the younger one does a jolly sight better. Now Paderewski and I——

WENTWORTH. Good heavens! I wish I hadn't started you on that. Get back to Bob. I thought Bob was on the Stock Exchange and Gerald in the Foreign Office. There can't be very much competition between them there.

TOMMY. Well, but there you are! Why isn't Bob in the Foreign Office and Gerald on the Stock Exchange? Why, because Gerald's the clever one, Gerald's the popular one, the good-looking one, the lucky one, the county cricketer, the plus three at golf——

WENTWORTH. Oh Lord! I thought you'd get golf into it. I suppose you were working up to your climax. Poor old Bob is about eighteen at golf, eh?

TOMMY. As a matter of fact, he's a very decent five. And there you are again. In any other family, Bob would be thought rather a nut. As it is——

WENTWORTH. As it is, Tommy, there are about thirty-five million people in England who've never played golf and who would recognize Bob, if they met him, for the decent English gentleman that he is.

TOMMY. I think you exaggerate, old chap. Golf's been getting awfully popular lately.

WENTWORTH. Personally I am very fond of Bob.

TOMMY. Oh, so am I. He's an absolute ripper. Still, *Gerald*, you know—I mean it's jolly bad luck on poor old Bob. Now Paderewski and I——

Enter GERALD *from the garden, a charming figure in a golfing coat and white flannels. Perhaps he is a little conscious of his charm; if so, it is hardly his fault, for hero-worship has been his lot from boyhood. He is now about twenty-six; everything that he has ever tried to do he has done well; and, if he is rather more unembarrassed than most of us when praised, his unself-consciousness is to a stranger as charming as the rest of him. With it all he is intensely reserved, with the result that those who refuse to succumb to his charm sometimes make the mistake of thinking that there is nothing behind it.*

GERALD. Hallo, Wentworth, how are you? All right?

WENTWORTH (*getting up and shaking hands*). Yes, thanks. How are you?

GERALD. Simply bursting. Have you seen your room and all that sort of thing?

WENTWORTH. Yes, thanks.

GERALD. Good. And Tommy's been entertaining you. (*To* TOMMY) Tommy, I interrupted your story about Paderewski. I don't think I know it. (*To* WENTWORTH) You must listen to this; it may be fairly new.

TOMMY. Don't be an ass. As a matter of fact, we were discussing something quite serious.

GERALD (*to* WENTWORTH). How long have you been here?

WENTWORTH. About ten minutes;

GERALD. And Tommy hasn't told you that he did the eighth in one this morning?

WENTWORTH. He hasn't really told me yet. He's only mentioned it once or twice in passing.

TOMMY (*modestly*). Well, I mean it's bound to appear in the papers, so naturally one——

GERALD. Oh, it's a great business. Champagne will flow like water to-night. There will also be speeches.

WENTWORTH. Which reminds me, Gerald, I have to congratulate you.

GERALD. Thank you very much. When you've seen her you'll want to do it again.

TOMMY (*looking through the window*). Hallo, there's Letty.

GERALD. If you want to tell her about it, run along, Tommy.

TOMMY (*moving off*). I thought I'd just take her on at putting.   [*He goes out.*

GERALD (*sitting down*). You'll stay till—well, how long can you? Tuesday, anyhow.

WENTWORTH. I think I can manage till Tuesday. Thanks very much. Miss Carey is here, of course?

GERALD. Yes, she'll be in directly. She's gone to the station to meet Bob.

WENTWORTH (*smiling*). And Gerald didn't go with her?

GERALD (*smiling*). At least six people suggested that Gerald should go with her. They suggested it very loudly and archly——

WENTWORTH. So Gerald didn't?

GERALD. So Gerald didn't. (*After a pause*) I can't stand that sort of thing.

WENTWORTH. What sort of thing?

GERALD (*after a pause*). Poor old boy! you've never been in love—barring the nine or ten times you're just going to tell me about. I mean never really in love.

WENTWORTH. Don't drag *me* into it. What is it you can't stand?

GERALD. People being tactful about Pamela and me. . . . Aunt Tabitha asked me yesterday if she might have Pamela for half an hour to do something or other —as if she were an umbrella, with my initials on it. . . . And somebody else said, "I've quite fallen in love with your Pamela; I hope you don't mind." *Mind?* I tell you, Wentworth, my boy, if you aren't in love with Pamela by Tuesday, there'll be the very deuce of a row. Your electro-plated butter-dish, or whatever it's going to be, will be simply flung back at you.

WENTWORTH. Well, as long as Miss Pamela understands——

GERALD. Of course she understands. We understand each other.

WENTWORTH (*preening himself*). Then I'll do my best. Mind, if she does happen to reciprocate my feelings, I wash my hands of all responsibility. (*Going towards the staircase*) Good-afternoon, Miss Farringdon.

MISS FARRINGDON *is coming slowly down the stairs.*

MISS FARRINGDON. Good-afternoon, Mr. Wentworth. Welcome.

> (*She must be well over eighty. She was pretty once, and sharp-tongued; so much you could swear to now. For the rest she is very, very wise, and intensely interested in life.*)

GERALD (*going over and kissing her*). Good-morning, Aunt Tabitha. Your chair is waiting for you. (*He conducts her to it.*)

MISS FARRINGDON. I'm a nasty cross old thing before

4

lunch, Mr. Wentworth, so I don't come down till afterwards nowadays. Is Gerald being as charming as usual?

WENTWORTH (*smiling*). Oh, pretty well.

GERALD (*looking at her lovingly and then turning to* WENTWORTH). It's having a very bad effect on her, this morning seclusion. She's supposed to be resting, but she spends her time trying to think of nasty things to say about me. The trouble with a mind like Aunt Tabitha's is that it can't think of anything *really* nasty.

MISS FARRINGDON. The trouble with Gerald, Mr. Wentworth, is that he goes about expecting everybody to love him. The result is that they nearly all do. However, he can't get round *me*.

GERALD. It isn't true, Wentworth; she adores me.

MISS FARRINGDON. He wouldn't be happy if he didn't think so.

WENTWORTH (*gracefully*). I can sympathize with him there.

GERALD. The slight coolness which you perceive to have arisen between my Aunt Tabitha and myself is due to the fact that I discovered her guilty secret a few days ago. For years she has pretended that her real name was Harriet. I have recently found out that she was christened Tabitha—or, anyhow, would have been, if the clergyman had known his job.

MISS FARRINGDON. My great-nephew, Gerald, Mr. Wentworth——

GERALD. *Nephew*, Wentworth. I agreed to waive the ' great " a long time ago.

WENTWORTH. You'll excuse my asking, but do you never talk to each other except through the medium of a third person?

MISS FARRINGDON (*to* GERALD). That's how they prefer to do it in the Foreign Office.   Isn't it, dear ?

GERALD. Always, Aunt Tabitha. But really, you know, we both ought to be talking to Wentworth and asking after his mother and his liver—and things like that.

MISS FARRINGDON. Yes, I'm afraid we're rather rude, Mr. Wentworth.   The Farringdons' great fault.

WENTWORTH (*protesting*). Oh no !

MISS FARRINGDON. How *is* Mrs. Wentworth ?

WENTWORTH. Wonderfully well, thank you, considering her age.

MISS FARRINGDON. Dear me, we met first in 1850.

GERALD. All frills and lavender.

MISS FARRINGDON. And now here's Gerald engaged. Have you seen Pamela yet ?

WENTWORTH. Not yet. I have been hearing about her from Tommy.   He classes her with the absolute rippers.

GERALD. Good old Tommy !

MISS FARRINGDON. Yes, she's much too good for Gerald.

GERALD. Of course she is, Aunt Tabitha. But if women only married men who were good enough for them, where should we be ?   As lots of young men said to you, in vain—on those afternoons when they read Tennyson aloud to you.

MISS FARRINGDON. She ought to have married Bob.

WENTWORTH (*surprised and amused*). Bob?   Is Bob good enough for her ?

MISS FARRINGDON. She would have made a good wife for Bob.

Enter suddenly LETTY HERBERT *and* TOMMY *from the garden.* LETTY *is an entirely delightful irresponsible girl of the type which might have shocked Queen Victoria. However, she seems to suit* TOMMY. *They are not engaged yet, but she has already that air of proprietorship.*

LETTY. I say, Tommy did the eighth in one. Why, there's Aunt Harriet. (*Going over and kissing her*) How are you, darling? Tommy's done the eighth in one. I know it doesn't mean much to you, but do say hooray, because he's so bucked about it.

GERALD (*to* WENTWORTH). Do you know Miss Herbert? Letty, come and be introduced. Mr. Wentworth—Miss Herbert.

LETTY (*shaking hands eagerly*). How do you do? I say, Tommy did the eighth in one. Do you know Tommy—*or* the eighth?

WENTWORTH. Both, Miss Herbert.

GERALD. To a man who knows both, the performance seems truly astonishing.

MISS FARRINGDON. I don't know anything about golf, Mr. Todd. But doing anything in one sounds rather clever. So I say hooray, too.

TOMMY. I wish you'd let me teach you, Miss Farringdon. Lots of people begin when they're frightfully old.

LETTY (*to* WENTWORTH). This is one of Tommy's polite days.

GERALD. Mr. Todd's famous old-world courtesy is the talk of many a *salon.*

MISS FARRINGDON (*to* TOMMY). Don't you mind them. I *am* frightfully old. I am very proud of it. I hope you'll all live to be as old as I am.

GERALD. I only hope we shall be half as nice.

MISS FARRINGDON. Gerald being charming as usual.

GERALD (*firmly*). I will also add that I hope we shall be kinder to our great-nephews than some.

LETTY (*putting her arm in his*). Diddums !

GERALD. Yes, I did. I am very much hurt.

TOMMY. I say, you know, Miss Farringdon, I never meant——

LETTY. I love Tommy when he apologizes.

Enter SIR JAMES *and* LADY FARRINGDON *from the door in front of the staircase.* SIR JAMES, *in a country check-suit, is a man of no particular brain and no ideas, but he has an unconquerable belief in himself, and a very genuine pride in, and admiration of,* GERALD. *His grey hair is bald on the top, and he is clean-shaven except for a hint of whisker. He might pass for a retired Captain R.N., and he has something of the quarter-deck manner, so that even a remark on the weather is listened to with attention. Neither of his sons loves him, but* GERALD *is no longer afraid of him.* LADY FARRINGDON *is outwardly rather intimidating, but she never feels so. She worships* GERALD ; *and would love a good many other people if they were not a little overawed by her.*

LADY FARRINGDON. Ah, you're here, Mr. Wentworth. How do you do ?

WENTWORTH (*coming forward*). How do you do, Lady Farringdon ? How do you do, Sir James ?

SIR JAMES. How are you, Wentworth ? Come to see Gerald play for the county *!*

GERALD. He's come to see Pamela. Haven't you, Wentworth ?

WENTWORTH. I rather hope to see both.

SIR JAMES. Ah, Aunt Harriet, I didn't see you. How are you to-day ?

MISS FARRINGDON. Very well, thank you, James. *He goes over to her.*)

LADY FARRINGDON. I hope they've shown you your room, Mr. Wentworth, and made you comfortable? Gerald, darling, you saw that Mr. Wentworth was all right?

WENTWORTH. Oh yes, that's quite all right, thank you, Lady Farringdon.

LADY FARRINGDON. Let me see, you're in the Blue Room, I think.

LETTY. It's much the nicest room to be in, Mr. Wentworth. There's a straight way down the water-pipe in case of fire.

GERALD. And a straight way up in case of burglars.

LADY FARRINGDON (*fondly*). Gerald, dear, don't be so foolish.

SIR JAMES. Gerald, is it true you went round in seventy-two?

GERALD. Yes. Tommy did the eighth in one.

TOMMY (*modestly*). Awful fluke.

SIR JAMES (*casually*). Ah—well done. (*To* GERALD) Seventy-two—that's pretty good. That's five under bogey, Mr. Wentworth.

LADY FARRINGDON (*to* WENTWORTH). Gerald has always been so good at everything. Even as a baby.

TOMMY. He did the ninth in three, Letty. How's that for hot?

SIR JAMES (*to* WENTWORTH). You must stay till Thursday, if you can, and see the whole of the Surrey match. It isn't often Gerald gets a chance of playing for the county now. It's difficult for him to get away from the Foreign Office. Lord Edward was telling me at the club the other day——

LETTY (*to* LADY FARRINGDON). Gerald dived off the Monk's Rock this morning. I'm glad I didn't see him. I should have been horribly frightened.

TOMMY (*proudly*). I saw him.

LETTY. Tommy, of course, slithered down over the limpets in the ordinary way.

LADY FARRINGDON (*fondly*). Oh, Gerald, how could you?

SIR JAMES (*still talking to* WENTWORTH). He tells me that Gerald is a marked man in the Service now.

TOMMY (*to* LETTY). Do you remember when Gerald——

MISS FARRINGDON (*incisively*). Let's *all* talk about Gerald.

> (GERALD, *who has been listening to all this with more amusement than embarrassment, gives a sudden shout of laughter.*)

GERALD. Oh, Aunt Tabitha, you're *too* lovely! (*He blows her a kiss and she shakes her stick at him.*)

Enter PAMELA *from the door in front of the staircase, tall, beautiful and serene, a born mother.* GERALD *carried her off her feet a month ago, but it is a question if he really touched her heart—a heart moved more readily by pity than by love.*

PAMELA. Gerald, dear, I'd know your laugh anywhere. Am I too late for the joke?

GERALD. Hullo, Pamela. Brought Bob with you?

PAMELA. He's just washing London off himself.

LADY FARRINGDON. Pamela, dear, do you know Mr. Wentworth?

PAMELA (*shaking hands*). How do you do?

LADY FARRINGDON (*to* WENTWORTH). Miss Carey— Gerald's Pamela.

PAMELA. I've heard so much about you, Mr. Wentworth.

WENTWORTH. And I've heard so much about you, Miss Carey.

PAMELA. That's nice.   Then we can start straight off as friends.

LETTY. I suppose you know Tommy did the eighth in one?

PAMELA. Rather.   It's splendid!

LETTY. *Do* say you haven't told Bob.

GERALD. Why shouldn't Bob know?

PAMELA. No, I haven't told him, Letty.

LETTY. Good, then Tommy can tell him.

TOMMY. They do pull my leg, don't they, Miss Farringdon?

Enter BOB *from the outer hall in a blue flannel suit.   He has spoilt any chance he had of being considered handsome by a sullen expression now habitual.   Two years older than Gerald, he is not so tall, but bigger, and altogether less graceful.   He has got in the way of talking in rather a surly voice, as if he suspected that any interest taken in him was merely a polite one.*

GERALD. Hullo, Bob; good man.

BOB. Hullo.   (*He goes up to* LADY FARRINGDON *and kisses her.*)   How are you, mother?

LADY FARRINGDON. It's so nice that you could get away, dear.

BOB. How are you, father?   All right?

SIR JAMES. Ah, Bob!   Come down to see your brother play for the county?

PAMELA (*quickly*). He's come down to see *me*, haven't you, Bob?

BOB. Hullo, Wentworth.   Hullo, Letty.   I say, I can't shake hands with you all.   (*He smacks* TOMMY *on the back and goes over to* MISS FARRINGDON.)   How are you, dear?

MISS FARRINGDON. Very glad to see my elder great-nephew.   I was getting tired of Gerald.

LADY FARRINGDON (*protesting*). Aunt Harriet, dear.

GERALD (*smiling*). It's all right, mother. We quite understand each other.

MISS FARRINGDON. I quite understand Gerald.

BOB. I say, aren't we going to have any tea?

LADY FARRINGDON. It's early yet, dear. Gerald, you'd like to have it outside, wouldn't you?

GERALD. Oh, rather. What do you say, Wentworth?

WENTWORTH. I never want to be indoors in the country if I can help it.

SIR JAMES. Quite right, Wentworth—quite right. Gerald, you'll just have time to take Wentworth round the stables before tea.

GERALD. You'll have to see them officially after church to-morrow. I don't know if you'd care about a private view now.

SIR JAMES. He must see your new mare. I should like to have his opinion of her.

WENTWORTH (*getting up*). I never know what to say to a mare, but I should like to come.

LETTY. She answers to " Hi !" or to any loud cry.

PAMELA. I'm sure you'll be all right, Mr. Wentworth.

GERALD. There's a way of putting one's head on one side and saying, " Ah !" Anybody who's seen Tommy at the Royal Academy will know exactly what I mean.

> (GERALD, PAMELA *and* WENTWORTH *move towards the door.*)

WENTWORTH (*to* PAMELA). Ought I to have a straw in my mouth?

GERALD. It's all right, we'll go and see the spaniels first.

WENTWORTH (*cheerfully*). Oh, I'm all right with dogs.

LETTY (*to* TOMMY). Come on, Tommy.

> [*They go out behind the others.*

LADY FARRINGDON. Would you like to have tea outside, Aunt Harriet?

MISS FARRINGDON. I'm not too old for that, Mary. Bob will bring me out. I want to have a word with him while I can. Everybody talks at once in this house.

SIR JAMES (*picking up his hat*). How's the City—hey?

BOB. Just as usual.

SIR JAMES. Coming round to the stables?

BOB. Later on, perhaps.

LADY FARRINGDON. Bob is bringing Aunt Harriet along, dear.

SIR JAMES. Ah, yes.   [*They go out together.*

MISS FARRINGDON. Smoke, Bob, and tell me how horrible the City is.

BOB (*lighting a pipe and sitting down*). It's damnable, Aunt Harriet.

MISS FARRINGDON. More damnable than usual?

BOB. Yes.

MISS FARRINGDON. Any particular reason why?

BOB (*after a long pause*). No.

> (MISS FARRINGDON *nods to herself and then speaks very casually.*)

MISS FARRINGDON. My bankers sent in my pass-book the other day. I seem to have a deal of money lying idle, as they call it. If anybody wanted it, I should really be in no hurry to get it back again.

BOB (*awkwardly*). Thanks very much. It isn't that. (*After a pause*) Not altogether.

MISS FARRINGDON. It was a great pity you ever went into the City, Bob.

BOB (*fiercely*). I could have told anybody that.

MISS FARRINGDON (*after waiting for him to say something more*). Well, suppose we go into the garden with the others. (*She begins to get up and he goes to help her.*) There's nothing you want to tell me, Bob?

BOB (*looking away*). What would there be?

MISS FARRINGDON. I'm a wise old woman, they say, and I don't talk.

BOB. I don't think you can help me.   Er—thanks very much.

MISS FARRINGDON (*quite naturally, as she turns towards the door*). If you don't mind giving me your arm.

> (*As they get to the door they are met by* GERALD *and* PAMELA *coming in.*)

GERALD. Hullo, Bob, we were just coming back for you.

MISS FARRINGDON. Thoughtful Gerald.

GERALD. Pamela's idea.   She thought that the elder members of the family could discuss life more freely unhampered by the younger generation.

PAMELA. What I really said was, " Where's Bob ?"

GERALD. Well, it's the same thing.

MISS FARRINGDON. Bob is looking after *me,* thank you very much.   [*They go out together.*

GERALD (*after watching them go, to* PAMELA). Stay here a bit.   There are too many people and dogs and things outside.   Come and sit on the sofa and I'll tell you all the news. (*He takes her hand and they go to the sofa together.*)   What ages you've been away !

PAMELA. An hour and a half.   And it need not have been that if you'd come with me.

GERALD (*taking her hand*). If I had come with you, I would have held your hand all the way.

PAMELA. I shouldn't have minded.

GERALD. But just think what would have happened. You would have had to have driven with one hand down all the hills ; we should have had a smash-up before we got halfway ; a well-known society beauty and a promising young gentleman in the Foreign Office would have been maimed for life ; and Bob would have to have walked here carrying his portmanteau. Besides, I love you going away from me when you come back. You've only got to come into the room, and the sun seems to shine.

PAMELA. The sun always shines on Gerald.

GERALD. Does it? That's a different sort of sunshine. Not the gentle caressing September afternoon sunshine which you wear all round you. (*She is looking at him lovingly and happily as he says this, but she withdraws into herself quickly as he pulls himself up and says with a sudden change of tone*) Dear me, I'm getting quite poetical, and two minutes ago I was talking to Wentworth about fetlocks.

PAMELA (*getting up*). Oh, Gerald, Gerald!

GERALD (*getting up and smiling at her*). Oh, Pamela Pamela!

PAMELA. I wonder how much you *really* want me.

GERALD. I'll show you when we're married. I don't think I could even begin to tell you now.

PAMELA (*wistfully*). Couldn't you try?

(GERALD *catches hold of her suddenly, and holding her tightly to him, kisses her again and again.*)

GERALD. There!

PAMELA (*releasing herself*). Oh, Gerald, my darling, you frighten me sometimes.

GERALD. Did I frighten you then?

PAMELA (*happily*). Oh, no, no, no, no! (*Earnestly*) Always want me very much, Gerald. Always be in need of me. Don't be too successful without me. However much the sun shines on you, let me make it gentler and more caressing for you.

GERALD. It is so, darling. Didn't I say so?

PAMELA. Ah, but I want such a lot of telling.

GERALD (*laughing happily as he goes over to the table by the fireplace and takes a cigarette*). Who was the fellow who threw something into the sea because he was frightened by his own luck? What shall I throw? (*Looking at a presentation clock on the mantelpiece*) That's rather asking for it. In a way it would be killing two birds with one stone. Oh, Lord, I am lucky!

PAMELA (*coming to him and taking his arm*). As long as you don't throw *me*.

GERALD. Pamela, you're talking rubbish. I talk a good deal myself, but I do keep within the bounds. Let's go and chatter to Bob about contangos. I don't know what they are, but they sound extraordinarily sober.

PAMELA (*gently*). Poor old Bob!

GERALD (*quickly*). Why *poor* old Bob?

PAMELA. He's worried about something. I tried to get him to tell me as we came from the station, but he wouldn't.

GERALD. Poor old Bob! I suppose things are going up—or down, or something. Brokerage one-eighth—that's what's worrying him, I expect.

PAMELA. I think he wants to talk to you about it. Be nice to him, darling, won't you?

GERALD (*surprised*). Nice to him?

PAMELA. You know what I mean—sympathetic. I know it's a difficult relationship—brothers.

GERALD. All relationships are difficult. But after you, he's the person I love best in the world. (*With a laugh*) But I don't propose to fall on his neck and tell him so.

PAMELA (*smiling*). I know you will help him if you can.

GERALD. Of course I will, though I don't quite see how. (*Hopefully*) Perhaps he's only slicing his drives again.

PAMELA. Oh, I love you, Gerald. (*Wonderingly*) *Do* I love you, or am I only just charmed by you?

GERALD. You said you loved me once.   You can't go back on that.

PAMELA. Then I love you.   And make a century for me on Monday.

GERALD. Well, I'll try.   Of course the bowler may be in love too.   But even if I get out first ball, I can say, " Well, anyhow, Pamela loves me."

PAMELA. Oh, I think I hope you get out first ball.

GERALD. Baby Pamela.

PAMELA. And on Thursday we shall be alone together here, and you've promised to take me out in the boat for the day.

GERALD. You mean you've promised to let me.

PAMELA. What happy days there are in the world !

Enter BOB *from the garden.*

GERALD. Hullo, Bob. Tea? (*He moves towards the door.*)

BOB. Cigarettes.   (*He goes over to the fireplace and fills his cigarette-case.*)

GERALD. Still, I expect tea's nearly ready.

PAMELA (*going towards door R. at the back*).   I'll join you ; I'm not going out without a sunshade again. [*Exit.*
(*There is an awkward silence.*)

BOB (*to* GERALD). I say !

GERALD (*turning round*). Hullo !

BOB. Just wait a moment.

(GERALD *comes back slowly.*)

GERALD. I warn you those are rotten cigarettes. (*Holds out his own case.*)

BOB (*taking one*). Thanks. (*Awkwardly*) You're so confoundedly difficult to get hold of nowadays.   Never less than half-a-dozen all round you.

GERALD (*laughing*). Good old Bob !

BOB (*after lighting a cigarette*). I want to talk to you about something.

GERALD. Well, of course.

BOB (*after a pause*). You've heard of Marcus, my partner?

GERALD (*with the idea of putting himself and* BOB *more at their ease*). Good old Marcus and Farringdon! It's the most perfect name for a firm. They sound so exactly as though they could sell you anything from a share to a shaving-brush. Marcus and Farringdon's pure badger, two shillings—gilt-edged badger half-a-crown.

BOB (*fiercely*). I suppose everything is just a pleasant joke to *you.*

GERALD (*utterly surprised*). Bob! Bob, old boy, what's the matter? (*Putting his hand on* BOB's *shoulder*) I say, Bob, I haven't hurt you, have I?

BOB (*hopelessly*). Oh, Jerry, I believe I'm in the devil of a hole.

GERALD. You haven't called me "Jerry" since we were at school.

BOB. You got me out of holes then—damn you! and you were my younger brother. Oh, Jerry, get me out of this one.

GERALD. But, of course. (*Firmly, as if a little nervous of a scene from* BOB) My dear Bob, you're as right as anything. You've got nothing on earth to worry about. At the worst it's only a question of money, and we can always put that right somehow.

BOB. I'm not sure that it *is* only a question of money.

GERALD (*frightened*). What do you mean? (*Turning away with a laugh*) You're talking nonsense.

BOB. Gerald, Marcus is a wrong un. (*Fiercely*) An out-and-out wrong un.

GERALD. The only time I saw him he looked like it.

BOB. God knows what he's let me in for.

GERALD. You mean money?

BOB. More than that, perhaps.

GERALD. You mean you're just going bankrupt?

BOB. No. (*After a pause*) Prosecution.

GERALD. Well, let them prosecute. That ends Marcus. You're well rid of him.

BOB (*miserably*). Perhaps it isn't only Marcus.

GERALD (*sharply, after this has sunk in*). What can they prosecute *you* for?

BOB (*speaking rapidly*). What the devil did they ever send me to the City for? I didn't want to go. I was never any good at figures. I loathe the whole thing. What the devil did they want to send me there for— and shove me on to a wrong un like Marcus? That's his life, messing about with money in the City. How can I stand out against a man like that? I never wanted to go into it at all.

GERALD (*holding out his cigarette-case*). Have another cigarette? (*They each light one, and* GERALD *sits down in the chair opposite to him.*) Let's look at it calmly. You've done nothing dishonourable, I know that. That's obvious.

BOB. You see, Jerry, I'm so hopeless at that sort of business. Naturally I got in the way of leaving things to Marcus. But that's all. (*Resentfully*) Of course, that's all.

GERALD. Good. Well, then, you're making much too much fuss about it. My dear boy, innocent people don't get put into prison nowadays. You've been reading detective stories. "The Stain on the Bath Mat," or "The Crimson Sponge." Good Lord! I shall be coming to *you* next and saying that *I'm* going to be put in prison for selling secret documents to a foreign country. These things don't happen; they don't really, old boy.

BOB (*cheered, but not convinced*). I don't know; it looks devilish bad, what I can make of it.

GERALD. Well, let's see what *I* can make of it.

BOB (*trying not to show his eagerness*). I was wondering if you would. Come up on Monday and we'll have a go at it together. Marcus has gone, of course. Probably halfway to South America by now. (*Bitterly*) Or wherever you go to.

GERALD. Right-o ! At least, I can't come on Monday, of course, but we'll have a go at it on Thursday.

BOB. Why can't you come on Monday ?

GERALD. Well, the Surrey match.

BOB (*bitterly*). I suppose as long as you beat Surrey, it doesn't matter if I go to prison.

GERALD (*annoyed*). Oh, shut up about going to prison ! There's not the slightest chance of your going to prison. You know perfectly well, if there were, that I'd walk on my hands and knees to London to-night to try and stop it As it is, I have promised to play for the county ; it's a particularly important match, and I don't think it's fair to let them down. Anyway, if I did, the whole family would want to know why, and I don't suppose you want to tell them that yet.

BOB (*mumbling*). You could say the Foreign Office had rung you up.

GERALD (*earnestly*). Really, Bob old boy, I'm sure you're making too much of it. Dammit ! you've done nothing wrong ; what is there to worry about ? And if it's only a question of money, we'll manage it on our heads, somehow. I'll come up directly the match is over. It may be Tuesday night, with luck.

BOB (*grumbling*). If the weather's like this, it's bound to last three days.

GERALD. Then at the worst, I'll come first train Thursday morning. That I promise. Anyway, why don't you consult Wentworth ? He's a good chap and

5

he knows all about the law. He could probably help you much more than I could.

BOB. I suppose you think I *like* talking about it to everybody.

GERALD (*getting up and touching* BOB *gently on the shoulder as he goes past him*). Poor old Bob ! But you're as right as anything. I'll come up by the first train on Thursday and we'll—good Lord !

BOB. What's the matter now ?

GERALD. I am a damned fool ! Why, of course, we arranged——

BOB (*sneeringly*). And now you can't come on Thursday, I suppose.

GERALD. Why, you see, I arranged——

BOB. You *must* keep your promise to the county, but you needn't keep your promise to me.

GERALD. Yes, but the trouble is I promised Pamela—oh, well, that will have to go ; she'll understand. All right, Bob, that holds. Directly the match is over I come. And for the Lord's sake, keep smiling till then.

BOB. It's all very well for *you*. . . . I wish you could have—well, anyhow, I suppose Thursday's better than nothing. You'll see just how it is then. (*Getting up*) You won't say anything about it to the others ?

GERALD. Of course not. What about Pamela ? Does she know anything ?

BOB. She knows that I'm worried about something, but of course she doesn't know what I've told you.

GERALD. All right, then I won't tell her anything. At least, I'll just say that bananas remain firm at 127, and that I've got to go and see my broker about it. (*Smiling*) Something like that.

> (BOB *goes towards the garden, while* GERALD *stops to wait for* PAMELA. *At the door he turns round.*)

BOB (*awkwardly*). Er—thanks.   [*Exit.*

(GERALD *throws him a nod, as much as to say,
"That's all right." He stands looking after
him, gives a little sigh, laughs and says to himself, "Poor old Bob!" He is half-sitting on,
half-leaning against the table, thinking it all
over, when* PAMELA *comes in again.*)

PAMELA. I waited for him to go; I knew he wanted
to talk to you about something.   Gerald, he is all right,
isn't he?

GERALD (*taking her hands*). Who? Bob? Oh yes,
he's all right.   So is Pamela.

PAMELA. Sure?

GERALD. Oh yes, he's all right.

PAMELA. I take rather a motherly interest in Bob, you
know.   What was worrying him?

GERALD (*smiling*). His arithmetic again; compound
interest.   His masters are very pleased with his progress in English.   And he wants more pocket-money.
He says that fourpence a week doesn't give him enough
scope.

PAMELA (*smiling*). But he really is all right?

GERALD. Well, I've got to go up on Thursday to see
his House Master—I mean I've got to go up to town on
Thursday.

PAMELA (*drawing back*). Thursday?   That was *our*
day, Gerald.

GERALD. Yes, I know ; it's a confounded nuisance.

PAMELA (*slowly*). Yes, it *is* rather a—nuisance.

GERALD. I'm awfully sorry, darling.   I hate it just as
much as you do.

PAMELA. I wonder if you do.

GERALD (*shaking his head at her*). Oh, woman, woman '
And you asked me to be kind to Bob.

PAMELA. It *is* for Bob?   He really does want you?

GERALD. He thinks I can help him if I go up on Thursday. (*Smiling*) We aren't going to quarrel about that.

PAMELA (*holding out her hand to him*). Come along. Of course we aren't going to quarrel—I don't think I could quarrel with you for more than five minutes. Only—you make me wonder sometimes.

GERALD (*getting up and taking her arm*). What do you wonder about?

PAMELA. Oh—things.

[*They go out into the garden together.*

ACT II

It is a quiet old-fashioned hotel which SIR JAMES *and* LADY
FARRINGDON *patronize in Dover Street on their occasional
visits to London. Their private sitting-room is furnished in heavy early Victorian style. A couple of
gloomy palms help to decorate the room, on whose walls
are engravings of Landseer's masterpieces.*

MASON, *a faithful kindly body, once nurse, now familiar
servant, is at the table arranging flowers, in a gallant
attempt to make the room more cheerful. As she fills
each vase she takes it to its place, steps back to consider
the effect, and returns to fill the next one.* GERALD, *in
London clothes as attractive as ever, but looking now
rather serious, discovers her at work.*

GERALD. Hullo, Nanny, when did you come?

MASON. This morning, sir. Her ladyship telegraphed
for me.

GERALD (*smiling affectionately at her*). Whenever there's
any trouble about, we send for Nanny. I wonder she
ever came to London without you.

MASON. I told her I'd better come, but she wouldn't
listen to me. Dear, dear! there *is* trouble about now
Master Gerald.

GERALD. Yes.

MASON. I thought a few flowers would cheer us up. I
said to Mr. Underhill before I started, "Give me some
flowers to take with me," I said, "so that I can make

59

the place look more homey and comfortable for her ladyship."

GERALD. And you have. No one like Nanny for that

MASON (*timidly*). Is there any news of Master Bob this morning? Of course, we've all been reading about it in the papers. They're not going to send him to prison?

GERALD. I'm afraid they are.

MASON. Dear, dear! (*She goes on arranging the flowers.*) He's not in prison now?

GERALD. No; he's on bail for the moment. Perhaps he'll be round here for lunch. But I'm afraid that to-night——

MASON. Even as a baby he was never quite like you, Master Gerald. Never was there such a little lamb as you. How long will they send him to prison for?

GERALD. We don't know yet; I expect we shall know this evening. But there's no doubt which way the case is going.

MASON. Two of the men were making their bets about it over the supper-table last night. I didn't wait long before giving them a piece of my mind, I can promise you.

GERALD (*turning round sharply*). Who were they? Out they go to-morrow.

MASON. That wouldn't be quite fair, would it, sir? They're young and thoughtless like.

GERALD (*to himself rather than to her*). After all, it's only what everybody else has been doing.

MASON. It wouldn't be anvthing very bad that Master Bob has done?

GERALD (*emphatically*). No, Nanny. No. Nothing bad; only—stupid.

MASON. I didn't know they put you in prison for being stupid. Some of us have been lucky.

GERALD. They can put you in prison for everything

Nanny—being stupid or being wise, being bad or being good, being poor or—yes, or being rich.

MASON (*putting her last touches to the flowers*). There! Now it looks much more like what her ladyship's used to. If you aren't sent to prison for being bad, it doesn't seem to matter so much.

GERALD. Well—it isn't nice, you know.

MASON. There's lots of things that aren't nice in the world. They haven't come *your* way yet, and I only hope they never will.

GERALD. I wish they hadn't come Bob's way.

MASON. Ah, Master Bob was born to meet them. Well, I'll go up to her ladyship now.

GERALD. Oh, are they back?

MASON. Sir James and her ladyship came back from the police-station——

GERALD. The Old Bailey, Nanny.

MASON. They came back about ten minutes ago, Master Gerald. And went up to their rooms.

GERALD. Tell mother I'm here, will you?

MASON. Yes, sir.

(*She goes out and comes back almost at once with* PAMELA.)

MASON. Here's Miss Pamela. (*To* PAMELA) I was just saying that her ladyship will be down directly.

GERALD (*smiling*). Not too directly now, Nanny.

MASON. No, Master Gerald. [*Exit.*

GERALD. Pamela! Have you just come up?

PAMELA. Mother and I are staying with Aunt Judith. Oh, Gerald! Poor, poor Bob!

GERALD. Have you seen him?

PAMELA. He came down to us last week, and he has been writing the most heart-rending letters.

GERALD. You're a dear to be so good to him.

PAMELA. How can one help it? Oh, Gerald, he *has*

been stupid! How he could have gone on as he did, hating it all, understanding nothing, but feeling all the time that things were wrong, and yet too proud or too obstinate to ask for help—hadn't you any idea, *any* of you?

GERALD (*awkwardly*). You never could get him to talk about the City at all. If you asked him, he changed the subject.

PAMELA (*reproachfully*). Ah! but how did you ask him? Lightly? Jokingly? "Hullo, Rothschild, how's the City getting on?" That sort of way. You didn't really mind.

GERALD (*smiling*). Well, if it comes to that, he didn't much mind how I was getting on at the Foreign Office. He never even said, "Hullo, Grey, how are Balkans?"

PAMELA. You had plenty of people to say that; Bob was different. I think I was the first person he really talked to about himself. That was before I met you. I begged him then to get out of it—little knowing. I wonder if it would have made any difference if you had gone up with him on—— Oh, well, it doesn't matter now.

GERALD (*defensively*). What were you going to say?

PAMELA. Nothing. (*Looking at him thoughtfully*) Poor Gerald! it's been bad for you too.

GERALD. You're not making it better by suggesting that I've let Bob down in some way—I don't quite know how.

PAMELA (*in distress*). Oh, Gerald, don't be angry with me—I don't want to hurt you. But I can only think of Bob now. You're so—you want so little; Bob wants so much. Why doesn't he come? I sent a note round to his rooms to say that I'd be here. Doesn't he have lunch here? Oh, Gerald, suppose the case is over, and they've taken him to prison, and I've never said good-bye to him. He said it wouldn't be over till this evening, but how would he know? Oh, I can't bear it if they've taken him away, and his only friend never said good-bye to him.

GERALD. Pamela, Pamela, don't be so silly. It's all right, dear; of course I'm not angry with you. And of course Bob will be here. I rang up Wentworth an hour ago, and he said the case can't end till this evening.

PAMELA (*recovering*). Sorry, Gerald, I'm being rather a fool.

GERALD (*taking her hands*). You're being—— (*There is a knock at the door, and he turns round impatiently*) Oh, what is it?

Enter MASON.

MASON (*handing note*). There's a telephone message been waiting for you, sir. And her ladyship will be down directly.

GERALD. Thank you, Nanny.   [*Exit* MASON. (*To* PAMELA) May I? (*He reads it*) Oh, I say, this is rather—this is from Wentworth. He's taken Bob round to lunch with him.

PAMELA (*going towards the door*). I must go, Gerald. Mr. Wentworth won't mind.

GERALD (*stopping her*). Look here, dear, it's going to be quite all right. Wentworth rang up from his rooms; they're probably halfway through lunch by now, and they'll be round in ten minutes.

PAMELA. Supposing he doesn't come? Supposing he didn't get my note? It may be waiting for him in his rooms now.

GERALD. All right, then, darling, I'll ring him up.

PAMELA (*determined*). No. I'll do it. Yes, Gerald, I know how to manage him. It isn't only that I must see

him myself, but if—(*bravely*) if the case is to be over
this evening, and if what we fear is going to happen, he
must—oh, he must say good-bye to his mother too.

GERALD. Well, if that's all, I'll tell him.

PAMELA. He mightn't come for you.   He will for me;
No, Gerald ; I mean it.   None of you understand him
I do.

GERALD. But supposing he's already started and you
miss him ?

PAMELA. I'll telephone to him at his rooms.   Oh,
don't stand there talking——

GERALD (*opening the door for her*). Oh, well !   But I
think you're——   [*She has gone.*

(*He walks up and down the room absently, picking up
papers and putting them down.* MASON *comes
in and arranges the sofa R.*)

MASON. Miss Pamela gone, Master Gerald ?

GERALD. She's coming back.

Enter LADY FARRINGDON.

LADY FARRINGDON. Oh, Gerald, I *hoped* you'd be here.

GERALD (*kissing her*). I've only just got away.   I
couldn't get round to the court. (*Seeing her to the sofa*)
You're all right, dear ?   [*Exit* MASON.

LADY FARRINGDON. Now you're here, Gerald.   I telegraphed for Mason.   She's such a comfort.   How nicely
she's done the flowers ! (*She sits down on the sofa.*)

GERALD. I'm so glad you sent for her.

LADY FARRINGDON. I don't think your father——

Enter SIR JAMES.

SIR JAMES. Ah, Gerald, I had to take your mother
out.   She was—ah—overcome.   They have adjourned,
I suppose ?

GERALD. Yes.   The judge is summing up directly

after lunch. Bob will be round here when he's had something to eat.

SIR JAMES (*looking at his watch*). Well, I suppose we ought to try and eat something.

LADY FARRINGDON. I couldn't touch anything.

GERALD (*going over to her*). Poor mother !

LADY FARRINGDON. Oh, Gerald, couldn't *you* do anything ? I'm sure if you'd gone into the witness-box, or told the judge—— Oh, why didn't you go to the Bar, and then you could have defended him. You would have been so much better than that stupid man.

SIR JAMES. I must say I didn't at all like his tone. He's practically making out my son to be an idiot.

GERALD. Well, it's really the only line he could take.

SIR JAMES. What do you mean ? Bob is far from being an idiot.

LADY FARRINGDON. We always knew he wasn't as clever as Gerald, dear.

GERALD. You see, Bob either understood what was going on or he didn't. If he did, then he's in it as much as Marcus. If he didn't—well, of course we know that he didn't. But no doubt the jury will think that he ought to have known.

SIR JAMES. The old story, a knave or a fool, eh ?

GERALD. The folly was in sending him there.

SIR JAMES (*angrily*). That was Parkinson's fault. It was he who recommended Marcus to me. I shall never speak to that man again. (*To his wife*) Mary, if the Parkinsons call, you are out ; remember that.

GERALD. He never ought to have gone into business at all. Why couldn't you have had him taught farming or estate agency or something ?

SIR JAMES. We've got to move with the times, my boy.

Land is played out as a living for gentlemen; they go into business nowadays. If he can't get on there, it's his own fault. He went to Eton and Oxford; what more does he want?

LADY FARRINGDON (*to* GERALD). You must remember he isn't clever like you, Gerald.

GERALD. Oh, well, it's no good talking about it now. Poor old Bob! Wentworth thinks——

SIR JAMES. Ah, now why couldn't Wentworth have defended him? That other man—why, to begin with, I don't even call him a gentleman.

GERALD. Wentworth recommended him. But I wish he had gone to Wentworth before, as soon as he knew what was coming.

SIR JAMES. Why didn't he come to *me*? Why didn't he come to *any* of us? Then we might have done something.

LADY FARRINGDON. Didn't he even tell *you*, Gerald?

GERALD (*awkwardly*). Only just at the last. It was— it was too late to do anything then. It was the Saturday before he was—arrested. (*To himself*) "The Saturday before Bob was arrested"—what a way to remember anything by!

LADY FARRINGDON (*to* GERALD). Bob is coming round, dear?

GERALD. Yes. Wentworth's looking after him. Pamela will be here too.

SIR JAMES. We haven't seen much of Pamela lately. What does *she* think about it?

GERALD (*sharply*). What do you mean

SIR JAMES. The disgrace of it. I hope it's not going to affect your engagement.

GERALD. Disgrace? what disgrace?

SIR JAMES. Well, of course, he hasn't been found guilty yet.

GERALD. What's that got to do with it? What does it matter what a lot of rotten jurymen think of him? *We* know that he has done nothing disgraceful.

LADY FARRINGDON. I'm sure Pamela wouldn't think anything like that of your brother, dear.

GERALD. Of course she wouldn't. She's been a perfect angel to Bob these last few weeks. What does it matter if he does go to prison?

SIR JAMES. I suppose you think I shall enjoy telling my neighbours, when they ask me what my elder boy is doing, that he's—ah—in prison.

GERALD. Of course you won't enjoy it, and I don't suppose Bob will enjoy it either, but that's no reason why we should make it worse for him by pretending that he's a disgrace to the family. (*Half to himself*) If anything we've done has helped to send him to prison then it's we who should be ashamed.

SIR JAMES. I don't profess to know anything about business, but I flatter myself that I understand my fellow men. If I had been in Bob's place, I should have pretty soon seen what that fellow Marcus was up to. I don't want to be unfair to Bob; I don't think that any son of mine would do a dishonourable action; but the Law is the Law, and if the Law sends Bob to prison I can't help feeling the disgrace of it.

GERALD. Yes, it's rough on you and mother.

LADY FARRINGDON. I don't mind about myself, dear. It's *you* I feel so sorry for—and Bob, of course.

GERALD. I don't see how it's going to affect *me*.

SIR JAMES. In the Foreign Office one has to be like Cæsar's wife—above suspicion.

GERALD. Yes, but in this case it's Cæsar's brother-in-law's partner who's the wrong un. I don't suppose Cæsar was so particular about *him*.

LADY FARRINGDON. I don't see how Cæsar comes into it at all.

SIR JAMES (*kindly*). I spoke in metaphors, dear.

The door opens and WENTWORTH *appears.*

GERALD. Come in, Wentworth. Where's Bob?

WENTWORTH. I dropped him at his rooms—a letter or something he wanted to get. But he'll be here directly. (*Nervously*) How do you do, Lady Farringdon? How do you do, Sir James?

SIR JAMES. Ah, Wentworth.

> (*There is an awkward silence and nobody seems to know what to say.*)

WENTWORTH. Very hot this morning.

SIR JAMES. Very hot. Very.

> (*There is another awkward silence.*)

WENTWORTH. This is quite a good hotel. My mother always stays here when she's in London.

SIR JAMES. Ah, yes. We use it a good deal ourselves.

LADY FARRINGDON. How *is* Mrs. Wentworth?

WENTWORTH. She's been keeping very well this summer, thank you.

LADY FARRINGDON. I'm so glad.

> (*There is another awkward silence.*)

GERALD (*impatiently*). Oh, what's the good of pretending this is a formal call, Wentworth? Tell us about Bob; how's he taking it?

WENTWORTH. He doesn't say much. He had lunch in my rooms—you got my message. He couldn't bear the thought of being recognized by anyone, so I had something sent up.

GERALD (*realizing what it must feel like*). Poor old Bob!

WENTWORTH. Lady Farringdon, I can't possibly tell you what I feel about this, but I should like to say that all of us who know Bob know that he couldn't do anything dishonourable. Whatever the result of the trial, we shall feel just the same towards him.

> (LADY FARRINGDON *is hardly able to acknowledge this, and* SIR JAMES *goes across to comfort her.*)

SIR JAMES (*helplessly*). There, there, Mary.

GERALD (*seizing his opportunity, to* WENTWORTH). What'll he get?

WENTWORTH (*quietly*). Three months—six months. One can't be certain.

GERALD (*cheering up*). Thank the Lord! I imagined awful things.

SIR JAMES (*his ministrations over*). After all, he hasn't been found guilty yet; eh, Wentworth?

WENTWORTH. Certainly, Sir James. With a jury there's always hope.

SIR JAMES. What do you think yourself?

WENTWORTH. I think he has been very foolish; whether the Law will call it criminally foolish I should hardly like to say. I only wish I had known about it before. He must have suspected something—didn't he say anything to anybody?

SIR JAMES. He told Gerald, apparently. For some reason he preferred to keep his father in the dark.

GERALD (*eagerly*). That was the day you came down to us, Wentworth; five days before he was arrested. I asked him to tell you, but he wouldn't.

WENTWORTH. Oh, it was too late *then*. Marcus had absconded by that time.

GERALD (*earnestly*). Nobody could have helped him then, could they?

WENTWORTH. Oh no.

GERALD (*to himself*). Thank God.

SIR JAMES (*to* LADY FARRINGDON *as he looks at his watch*). Well, dear, I really think you ought to try to eat something.

LADY FARRINGDON. I couldn't, James. (*Getting up*)
But you must have *your* lunch.

SIR JAMES. Well, one oughtn't to neglect one's health,
of course. But I insist on your having a glass of claret
anyhow, Mary. What about you, Gerald?

GERALD. I'm all right. I'll wait for Bob. I've had
something.

LADY FARRINGDON. You won't let Bob go without
seeing us?

GERALD. Of course not, dear.

(*He goes with them to the door and sees them out.*)

GERALD (*coming back to* WENTWORTH). Three months.
By Jove! that's nothing.

WENTWORTH. It's long enough for a man with a
grievance. It gives him plenty of time to brood about it.

GERALD (*anxiously*). Who has Bob got a grievance
against particularly?

WENTWORTH. The world.

GERALD (*relieved*). Ah! Still, three months, Wentworth. I could do it on my head.

WENTWORTH. You're not Bob. Bob will do it on his
heart.

GERALD. We must buck him up, Wentworth. If he
takes it the right way, it's nothing. I had awful
thoughts of five years.

WENTWORTH. I'm not the judge, you know. It may
be six months.

GERALD. Of course. How does he decide? Tosses
up for it? Three months or six months or six years,
it's all the same to him, and there's the poor devil in
the dock praying his soul out that he'll hit on the
shortest one. Good Lord! I'm glad I'm not a judge.

WENTWORTH (*drily*). Yes; that isn't quite the way
the Law works.

GERALD. Oh, I'm not blaming the Law. (*Smiling*)

Stick to it, Wentworth, by all means. But I should make a bad judge. I should believe everything the prisoner said, and just tell him not to do it again.

BOB *comes in awkwardly and stops at the door.*

WENTWORTH (*getting up*). Come along, Bob. (*Taking out his case*) Have a cigarette.

BOB (*gruffly*). No, thanks. (*He takes out his pipe.*)

GERALD (*brightly but awkwardly*). Hullo, Bob, old boy.

BOB. Where's Pamela? She said she'd be here. (*He sits down in the large armchair.*)

GERALD. If she said she'd be here, she will be here.

BOB (*with a grunt*). 'M! (*There is an awkward silence.*)

BOB (*angrily to* GERALD). Why don't you say something? You came here to say good-bye to me, I suppose—why don't you say it?

WENTWORTH. Steady, Bob.

GERALD (*eagerly*). Look here, Bob, old son, you mustn't take it too hardly. Wentworth thinks it will only be three months—don't you, Wentworth? You know, we none of us think any the worse of you for it.

BOB. Thanks. That will console me a lot in prison.

GERALD. Oh, Bob, don't be an old fool. You know what I mean. You have done nothing to be ashamed of, so what's the good of brooding in prison, and grousing about your bad luck, and all that sort of thing? If you had three months in bed with a broken leg, you'd try and get *some* sort of satisfaction out of it—well, so you can now if you try.

WENTWORTH (*after waiting for* BOB *to say something*). There's a good deal in that, Bob, you know. Prison is largely what you make it.

BOB. What do either of you know about it?

GERALD. Everything. The man with imagination knows the best and the worst of everything.

6

BOB (*fiercely*). Imagination ? You think *I* haven't imagined it ?

GERALD. Wentworth's right. You can make what you like of it. You can be miserable anywhere, if you let yourself be. You can be happy anywhere, if you try to be.

WENTWORTH (*to lead him on*). I can't quite see myself being actually happy in prison, Gerald.

GERALD. I could, Wentworth, I swear I could.

BOB. He'd get popular with the warders; he'd love that.

GERALD (*smiling*). Silly old ass ! But there are lots of things one can do in prison, only no one ever seems to think of them. (*He gets interested and begins to walk up and down the room.*) Now take this solitary confinement there's so much fuss about. If you look at it the right way, there's nothing in it at all.

WENTWORTH. A bit boring, perhaps.

GERALD. Boring ? Nonsense. You're allowed one book a week from the prison library, aren't you ?

WENTWORTH. You know, you mustn't think that, because I'm a barrister, I know all about the inside of a prison.

GERALD. Well, suppose you are allowed one, and you choose a French dictionary, and try to learn it off by heart before you come out. Why, it's the chance of a lifetime to learn French.

WENTWORTH. Well, of course, if you *could* get a French dictionary——

GERALD. Well, there 'd be *some* book there anyway If it's a Bible, read it. When you've read it, count the letters in it ; have little bets with yourself as to which man's name is mentioned most times in it ; put your money on Moses and see if you win. Anything like that. If it's a hymn-book, count how many of the rhymes rhyme and how many don't; try and make them *all* rhyme. Learn 'em by heart; I don't say that that would be particularly useful to you in the business world afterwards, but it would be amusing to see how quickly you could do it, how many you could keep in your head at the same time.

WENTWORTH. This is too intellectual for me; my brain would go in no time.

GERALD. You aren't doing it all day, of course; there are other things. Physical training. Swedish exercises. Tell yourself that you'll be able to push up fifty times from the ground before you come out. Learn to walk on your hands. Practise cart-wheels, if you like. Gad you could come out a Hercules.

WENTWORTH. I can't help feeling that the strain of improving myself so enormously would tell on me.

GERALD. Oh, you'd have your games and so on to keep you bright and jolly.

WENTWORTH (*sarcastically*). Golf and cricket, I suppose?

GERALD. Golf, of course; I'm doubtful about cricket You must have another one for cricket, and I'm afraid the warder wouldn't play. But golf, and squash rackets, and bowls, and billiards—and croquet——

WENTWORTH (*in despair*). Oh, *go* on !

GERALD. Really, you're hopeless. What the Swiss Family Wentworth would have done if they'd ever been shipwrecked, I can't think. Don't you *ever* invent *any*thing for yourself? (*Excitedly*) Man alive ! you've got a hymn-book and a piece of soap, what more do you want? You can play anything with that. (*Thoughtfully*) Oh, I forgot the Olympic games. Standing long jump. And they talk about the boredom of it !

WENTWORTH (*thoughtfully*). You've got your ideas, Gerald. I wonder if you'd act up to them.

GERALD. One never knows, but honestly I think so.

(*There is silence for a little.*)

BOB. Is that all?

GERALD. Oh, Bob, I know it's easy for me to talk——

BOB. I wonder you didn't say at once: "Try not to think about it." You're always helpful.

GERALD. You're a little difficult to help, you know Bob. (*Awkwardly*) I thought I might just give you an idea. If I only could help you, you know how——

BOB (*doggedly*). I asked you to help me once.

GERALD (*distressed*). Oh, I didn't realize then—besides, Wentworth says it would have been much too late—didn't you, Wentworth?

WENTWORTH (*taking up his hat*). I think I must be getting along now. (*Holding out his hand*) Good-bye, Bob. I can only say, "The best of luck," and—er—whatever happens, you know what I feel about it.

BOB (*shaking his hand*). Good-bye, Wentworth, and thanks very much for all you've done for me.

WENTWORTH (*hurriedly*). That's all right. (*To* GERALD, *quietly, as he passes him on the way to the door*) You must bear with him, Gerald. Naturally he's—— (*Nodding*) Good-bye.   [*He goes out.*

GERALD (*going back to* BOB). Bob——

BOB. Why doesn't Pamela come? I want Pamela.

GERALD (*speaking quickly*). Look here, think what you like of me for the moment. But you must listen to what I've got to say. You can imagine it's somebody else speaking—Pamela, if you like—Pamela would say just the same. You *must not* go to prison and spend your time there brooding over the wrongs people have done to you, and the way the world has treated you, and all that sort of thing. You simply must make an effort—and—and—well, come out as good a man as you went in. I know it's easy for me to talk, but that doesn't make it

any the less true. Oh, Bob, be a—be a Sportsman
about it! You can take it out of me afterwards, if you
like, but don't take it out of me now by—by not
bucking up just because I suggest it.

BOB. I want Pamela. Why doesn't she come?

(PAMELA *has come in while he is saying this.*)

PAMELA. Here I am, Bob.

BOB (*getting up*). At last! I began to be afraid you
were never coming.

PAMELA. You couldn't think that. I told you I was
coming.

GERALD. Look here, Pamela, we've got to cheer old
Bob up.

BOB (*almost shouting*). Good Lord! can't you see that
I don't want *you*? I want Pamela alone.

PAMELA (*putting her hand on* GERALD's *shoulder*). Gerald,
dear, you mustn't be angry with Bob now. Let me be
alone with him.

GERALD (*with a shrug*). All right. Poor old Bob!
(*He goes over to his brother and holds out his hand.*) Good-
bye, old boy, and—good luck.

BOB (*coldly*). Good-bye.

GERALD. Shake hands, Bob.

BOB. No. I've been nothing to you all your life.
You could have saved me from this, and you wouldn't
help me.

GERALD (*angrily*). Don't talk such rot!

PAMELA (*coming between them*). Gerald, dear, you'd
better go. Bob won't always feel like this towards you,
but just now——

GERALD (*indignantly*). Pamela, *you* don't believe this
about me?

PAMELA. I can't think of *you*, dear, now; I can only
think of Bob.   [GERALD *gives a shrug and goes out.*

BOB. Pamela.

PAMELA (*coming to him*). Yes, dear ?

BOB. Come and sit near me. You're the only friend I've got in the world.

PAMELA. You know that isn't true.

(*She sits down in the armchair and he sits on the floor at her feet.*)

BOB. If it hadn't been for you, I should have shot myself long ago.

PAMELA. That would have been rather cowardly, wouldn't it ?

BOB. I am a coward. There's something about the Law that makes people cowards. It's so—what's the word ? It goes on. You can't stop it, you can't explain to it, you can't even speak to it.

PAMELA. But you can stand up to it. You needn't run away from it.

BOB. I think I would have broken my bail and run, if it hadn't been for you. But you would have thought less of me if I had. Besides, I shouldn't have seen you again.

PAMELA. Bob, you mustn't just do, or not do, things for *me ;* you must do them because of yourself. You must be brave because it's you, and honourable because it's you, and cheerful because it's you. You mustn't just say, " I won't let Pamela down." You must say, " I won't let myself down." You must be proud of yourself.

BOB (*bitterly*). I've been taught to be proud of myself, haven't I ? Proud of myself ! What's the family creed ? " I believe in Gerald. I believe in Gerald the Brother. I believe in Gerald the Son. I believe in Gerald the Nephew. I believe in Gerald the Friend, the Lover Gerald the Holy Marvel." There may be brothers who don't mind that sort of thing, but not when you're born jealous as I was. Do you think father or mother cares a damn what happens to me ? They're

upset, of course, and they feel the disgrace for them-
selves, but the belovèd Gerald is all right, and that's all
that really matters.

PAMELA. Bob, dear, forget about Gerald now. Don't
think about him ; think about yourself.

BOB. I shan't think about myself or about Gerald
when I'm in prison. I shall only think of you.

PAMELA. Will it help you to think of me?

BOB. You're the only person in the world I've got
to think of. I found you first—and then Gerald took
you from me. Just as he's always taken everything
from me.

PAMELA. No, no. Not about Gerald again. Let's get
away from Gerald.

BOB. You can't. He's a devil to get away from.
(*There is silence for a little.*) When I was a small boy,
I used to pray very hard on the last day of the holidays
for a telegram to come saying that the school had been
burnt down. . . . It never had.

PAMELA. Oh, Bob !

BOB. I suppose I've got about ten minutes more.
But nothing will happen.

PAMELA (*in a hopeless effort to be hopeful*). Perhaps
after all you might——

BOB. Why can't the world end suddenly now ? It
wouldn't matter to anybody. They wouldn't know ;
they wouldn't have time to understand. (*He looks up
and sees her face of distress and says*) All right, Pamela,
you needn't worry. I'm going through with it all
right.

PAMELA. You must keep thinking of the afterwards.
Only of the afterwards. The day when you come
back to us.

BOB. Will that be such a very great day ? (PAMELA
is silent.) Triumphant procession through the village.

All the neighbours hurrying out to welcome the young squire home. Great rush in the City to offer him partnerships.

PAMELA (*quietly*). Do you want to go back to the City?

BOB. Good God, no!

PAMELA. Then why are you being sarcastic about it? Be honest with yourself, Bob. You made a mess of the City. Oh, I know you weren't suited to it, but men have had to do work they didn't like before now, and they haven't *all* made a mess of it. You're getting your punishment now—much more than you deserve, and we're all sorry for you—but men have been punished unfairly before now and they have stood it. You'll have your chance when you come back; I'll stand by you for one, and you've plenty of other friends; but we can't help a man who won't help himself, you know.

BOB (*sulkily*). Thank you, Pamela.

PAMELA (*shaking him*). Bob, Bob, don't be such a baby. Oh, I want to laugh at you, and yet my heart just aches for you. You're just a little boy, Bob (*with a sigh*), on the last day of his holidays.

BOB (*after a pause*). Are you allowed to have letters in prison?

PAMELA. I expect so. Every now and then.

BOB. You will write to me?

PAMELA. Of course, dear; whenever I may.

BOB. I suppose some beast will read it. But you won't mind that, will you?

PAMELA. No, dear.

BOB. I'll write to you whenever they let me. That will be something to look forward to. Will you meet me when I come out?

PAMELA (*happily*). Yes, Bob. So very gladly.

BOB. I'll let you know when it is. I expect I'll be allowed to.

PAMELA. You must just think of that day all the time Whenever you are unhappy or depressed or angry, you must look forward to that day.

BOB. You'll let it be a fine day, won't you? What shall we do?

PAMELA (*rather startled*). What?

BOB. What shall we do directly after I come out?

PAMELA. Well, I suppose we—I mean you—well, we'll come up to London together, I suppose, and you'll go to your old rooms. At least, if you still have them.

BOB (*instantly depressed again*). My old rooms. That'll be lively.

PAMELA. Well, unless you'd rather——

BOB. I'm not going home, if that's what you mean. The prodigal son, and Gerald falling on my neck.

PAMELA (*stroking his head*). Never mind Gerald, Baby
(*He turns round suddenly and seizes her hands.*)

BOB (*in a rush*). Whatever happens, you mustn't desert me when I come out. I want you. I've got to know you're there, waiting for me. I'm not making love to you, you're engaged to somebody else, but you were my friend before you were his, and you've got to go on being my friend. I want you—I want you more than he does. I'm not making love to you; you can marry him if you like, but you've got to stand by me. I want you.

PAMELA. Haven't I stood by you?

BOB (*in a low voice*). You've been an angel. (*He kisses her hands and then gets up and walks away from her; with his back to her, looking out of the window, he says*) When are you marrying him?

PAMELA (*taken by surprise*). I—I don't know, Bob.

We *had* thought about—but, of course, things are different now.   We haven't talked about it lately.

BOB (*casually*). I wonder if you'd mind promising me something.

PAMELA. What is it?

BOB. Not to get married till after I come out.   (*After waiting for* PAMELA *to speak*) You will have about forty years together afterwards.   It isn't much to ask.

PAMELA. Why should it make a difference to you?

BOB. It would.

PAMELA. It isn't a thing I like making promises about. But I don't suppose for a moment—— Would it help you very much, Bob?

BOB (*from the bottom of his heart*). I don't want Gerald's wife to be waiting for me when I come out; I want *my friend*.

PAMELA (*standing up and facing him as he turns round towards her*). All right, Bob, she shall be there.

> (*They stand looking at each other intently for a moment.   Voices are heard outside, and* SIR JAMES, LADY FARRINGDON, *and* GERALD *come into the room.*)

ACT III

SCENE.—*In the hall at* SIR JAMES FARRINGDON'S *again. It is autumn now and there is a fire burning.*

LETTY *and* TOMMY *are on the sofa side by side, holding hands, and looking the picture of peaceful happiness. Indeed,* TOMMY *has his mouth open slightly.*

LETTY. It's your turn to say something, Tommy.

TOMMY. Oh, I say.

LETTY. Now I suppose it's my turn.

TOMMY. I say, you know, I feel too idiotically happy to say anything. I feel I want to talk poetry, or rot like that, only—only I don't quite know how to put it.

LETTY (*sympathetically*). Never mind, darling.

TOMMY. I say, you do understand how frightfully—I say, what about another kiss ? (*They have one.*)

LETTY. Tommy, I just adore you. Only I think you might have been a little more romantic about your proposal.

TOMMY (*anxious*). I say, do you——

LETTY. Yes. Strictly speaking, I don't think anybody ought to propose with a niblick in his hand.

TOMMY. It just sort of came then. Of course I ought to have put it down.

LETTY. You dear ! . . . " Letting his niblick go for a moment, Mr. T. Todd went on as follows : ' Letitia, my belovèd, many moons have waxed and waned since first

81

I cast eyes of love upon thee. An absence of ducats, coupled with the necessity of getting my handicap down to ten, has prevented my speaking ere this. Now at last I am free. My agèd uncle——'"

TOMMY (*lovingly*). I say, you do pull my leg. Go on doing it always, won't you?

LETTY. Always, Tommy. We're going to have fun, always.

TOMMY. I'm awfully glad we got engaged down here.

LETTY. We've had lovely times here, haven't we?

TOMMY. I wonder what Gerald will say. A bit of a surprise for him. I say, it would be rather fun if we had a double wedding. You and I, and Gerald and Pamela.

LETTY (*getting up in pretended indignation*). Certainly not!

TOMMY (*following her*). I say, what's the matter?

LETTY (*waving him back*). Go away. Unhand me villain.

TOMMY. I say, what's up?

LETTY. I want a wedding of my own. I've never been married before, and perhaps I shall never be married again, and I'm going to have a wedding all to myself. I don't mind your being there, but I'm not going to have crowds of other brides and bridegrooms taking up the whole aisle—said she, seizing her engagement-ring and—— Oh, bother! I haven't got one yet.

> (TOMMY *rushes up and takes her in his arms. At this moment* GERALD *comes in by the garden door. He stops on seeing them, and then goes quickly on to the door in front of the staircase.*)

GERALD (*as he passes them*). Came in and went tactfully out again.

TOMMY (*as* LETTY *frees herself*). I say, Gerald, old man.

GERALD (*stopping at the door, turning round and coming back in the same business-like way*). Returned hopefully.

TOMMY (*in confusion*). I say, we're engaged.

GERALD (*looking at them happily*). Oh, hoo-ray !

LETTY. *Do* say you're surprised.

GERALD. Awfully, awfully pleased, Letty. Of course, when I saw you—er—thinking together in a corner I—— By Jove, I *am* bucked. I did hope so much.

LETTY. You dear !

GERALD. I feel very fatherly. Bless you, my children.

TOMMY. We shall have about tuppence a year, but Letty doesn't mind that.

GERALD (*to* LETTY). You'll have to make him work. (*Thoughtfully*) He's too old for a caddy.

LETTY. Couldn't you find him something in the Foreign Office ? He knows the French for pen and ink.

TOMMY. What's ink ?

LETTY. At least, he knows the French for pen.

GERALD. Oh, we'll find something. Only I warn you, Tommy, if you dare to get married before Pamela and me, there'll be trouble.

TOMMY. Why don't we ever see Pamela now ?

GERALD (*gaily*). She is coming, my children—*mes enfants*, as Tommy will say when he gets his job as ribbon starcher to the French ambassador. To-morrow, no less. I've just had a letter. Lord, I haven't seen her for months.

LETTY. She's come back ?

GERALD. Yes. Egypt knows her no more. The Sphinx is inconsolable. To-morrow at 3.30 she comes ; I shall go and meet her.

TOMMY. I say, won't she be surprised about Letty and me !

GERALD. She'll be as bucked as I am. (*Looking from one to the other*) Has anything else frightfully exciting happened to you since lunch ? Because, if not, I've got some more news.

LETTY. What is it? I love news.

GERALD. All ready? Then one, two, three: Bob is coming this afternoon.

LETTY }
and } (*together*). No!
TOMMY } Rot!

GERALD (*singing to the tune of "Here we go gathering nuts and may"*). Oh, Bob is coming this afternoon, this afternoon, this afternoon! Oh, Bob is coming this afternoon, all on an autumn morning! Now then, all together.

(*They join hands and march up the hall and back again, singing together.*)

ALL TOGETHER (*waving imaginary hats*). Hooray! Hooray! Hooray!

TOMMY. It doesn't make sense, you know, coming back in the afternoon on an autumn morning.

GERALD. Who cares for sense?

LETTY (*squeezing his arm*). Oh, Gerald, I *am* glad. But I thought he had another week or so.

GERALD. They always let you out early, you know, if you're good. We knew he was coming soon, but we didn't quite know when. I've just had a telegram.

LETTY. Poor Bob! he must have had a time.

GERALD. What does it matter? It's over now.

TOMMY (*struck by an idea*). I say, this puts a bit of a stopper on *our* news.

GERALD (*pulled up suddenly by this*). Oh!

LETTY (*going over and taking* TOMMY'S *arm*). We'll go to a house where they *do* make a fuss of us, Tommy. (*Very politely*) Good-bye, Mr. Farringdon, and thank you for a very pleasant Friday.

GERALD. Poor darlings! it's rather bad luck for you. Did I announce my news too soon? I'm awfully sorry.

LETTY. It wasn't your fault; you were a dear.

GERALD. As a matter of fact, it will be rather lucky, you know. It will give us something to talk about when Bob comes. (*Smiling*) Thanks very much for arranging it.

LETTY. Poor old Bob! I wonder what it feels like coming out of prison.

GERALD. Rotten. Now, for the Lord's sake, Tommy, be tactful.

LETTY (*to* GERALD). I think he'd be safer if he wasn't Tommy's rather dangerous when he's tactful.

GERALD (*thoughtfully*). Yes, there *is* that.

TOMMY. It's all the same to me. Only just let me know which you want.

GERALD. Well, as long as you don't overdo it. Don't rub it in that he's just left prison, and—don't rub it out.

TOMMY. I suppose it would be quite safe to ask him to pass the mustard?

GERALD (*laughing*). Good old Tommy!

LETTY. You'd better talk to *me* all the time, and then you'll be all right.

GERALD. We'll make it go between us. And, of course, Pamela will help to-morrow. Hooray for Pamela! It makes me quite envious seeing you young people together. By the way, I interrupted you just now.

LETTY. You did rather.

GERALD. Well, I absolutely refuse to go away now. But, of course, if you're longing to show each other the stables or anything—(*with a wave of the hand*) pray show. Or try anywhere else. Save for Aunt Tabitha's room upstairs and the hall down here, the whole house is at your disposal.

LETTY (*sitting down firmly*). Then I shall stay here. Isn't Aunt Mary back yet?

GERALD. They are probably still eating. It's the very

latest millionaire from London, so they're having the lunch of their lives, I expect. Afterwards father will put him at his ease by talking about crops. (*Picking up a book and settling himself comfortably in front of the fire*) Tommy, if you can't find a book, sing or something.

LETTY. Oh, come on, Tommy.

> [*She jumps up and goes out of the door in front of the staircase*, TOMMY *following her*.

> (*Left alone,* GERALD *closes his book with a slam. He stands up and takes the telegram out of his pocket and reads it again. He suddenly catches sight of* MISS FARRINGDON *in the gallery above, calls out "Hullo!" and goes up the stairs to meet her.*)

GERALD (*as he goes*). You're just the person I wanted, Aunt Tabitha. I'm full of news. (*He kisses her at the top of the stairs.*) How are you, dear? (*He offers her his arm.*)

MISS FARRINGDON. If I had wanted help down the stairs, Gerald, my maid could have given it me.

GERALD. Yes, but your maid wouldn't have enjoyed giving it you; I do.

MISS FARRINGDON. Charming Gerald. (*She comes down the stairs on his arm.*)

GERALD. No, happy Gerald.

MISS FARRINGDON. Is that part of the news?

GERALD. It's all because of the news.

> (*He arranges her in her chair by the fire and sits on the coffin-stool near her.*)

MISS FARRINGDON. I heard Mr. Todd and Letty just now, so I suppose I shan't be the first to hear it. What a pity!

GERALD. Ah, but they don't count.

MISS FARRINGDON. Why not?

GERALD. Well, that's part of the news. They've just got engaged.

MISS FARRINGDON. In my young days they'd have been engaged a long time ago. When are we going to see Pamela again?

GERALD. That's more of the news. She's coming down to-morrow.

MISS FARRINGDON. That will save you a lot in stamps.

GERALD (*laughing*). Aunt Tabitha, you're a witch How did you know?

MISS FARRINGDON. Know what?

GERALD. That Pamela and I haven't been writing to each other.

MISS FARRINGDON (*very innocently*). Haven't you?

GERALD. No. You see—oh, I hate discussing Pamela with anyone, but you're different.

MISS FARRINGDON. I always like that sort of compliment best, Gerald. The unintended sort.

GERALD. I think, you know, Pamela felt that Bob's going to prison might make a difference. I don't mean that she didn't like the disgrace for herself, but that she was afraid that I mightn't like it for her; and so she went away, and beyond a letter or two at the start there hasn't been a Pamela.

MISS FARRINGDON. But Gerald went on being successful?

GERALD. Oh, Aunt Tabitha, Aunt Tabitha, if ever I were going to be conceited—and I don't think I am really—you'd soon stop it, wouldn't you? I wonder if you *do* know me as well as you think. You think I'm all outside, don't you, and inside there's nothing?

MISS FARRINGDON. Oh, you've got brains, I'll grant you that. You're the first Farringdon that's had any. Of the men, of course.

GERALD. Oh, brains—I don't mean brains. But you think that everything only touches me on the surface, and that nothing ever goes deep inside. You don't

7

believe I ever loved Pamela ; you don't believe I love her now. You don't believe I've got a heart at all.

MISS FARRINGDON. Well, you've never shown it. You've shown a lot of delightful things which silly people mistake for it—but that's all.

GERALD (*curtly*). No, I've never shown my heart to anybody. Some people can't. (*Gently*) Perhaps I'll show it to Pamela on my wedding-day.

MISS FARRINGDON. Dear me, have I been wrong all these years ? I shouldn't like to think that. (*After a pause*) Any more news ?

GERALD (*taking his thoughts off* PAMELA). Yes. Now *this* time, Aunt Tabitha, you'll really be as pleased as I am.

MISS FARRINGDON. I wonder.

GERALD. Oh yes, you will, because it's about your favourite—Bob.

MISS FARRINGDON. So Bob's my favourite ? I'm learning a good many things to-day.

GERALD. He's coming back this afternoon.

MISS FARRINGDON. Poor Bob ! I'm glad he's finished with that part of it.

GERALD. You think he's got the worst part coming ? (*Smiling at her*) Aunt Tabitha, have you got any influence with your nephew ?

MISS FARRINGDON. You or Bob ? (GERALD *smiles and shakes his head.*) Oh, you mean James ?

GERALD. It seems hard to realize that one's father is anybody else's nephew, but you *are* his aunt, and—— Oh, don't let him do anything stupid about Bob.

MISS FARRINGDON. Bob's his own master ; he's old enough to look after himself.

GERALD. Yes, but he's got in the way of being looked after by other people. I wish *you* would look after him and tell him what to do. It's going to be difficult for him. I expect he'll want to get away from all of us for a bit. Where's he going, and what's he going to do?

MISS FARRINGDON (*after a pause*). When did you say Pamela was coming here?

GERALD. To-morrow. *She'll* help, of course.

MISS FARRINGDON. Gerald, you've been very nice to me always; I don't know why I've been rather unkind to you sometimes.

GERALD. What an idea! You know I've loved our little skirmishes.

MISS FARRINGDON. That's because you've been happy, and haven't minded one way or another. But if ever you were in trouble, Gerald, I don't think I should be unsympathetic.

GERALD. You dear, of course you wouldn't. But why do you say that now, just when I *am* so happy?

MISS FARRINGDON (*getting up slowly*). I'm feeling rather an old woman to-day. I think I'll go and lie down.

GERALD (*jumping up*). I'll ring for your maid.

MISS FARRINGDON. No, no; I'm not going upstairs, and I don't want a maid when I've got a great big nephew. Come and tuck me up on the sofa in the drawing-room; I shall be quite happy there.

> (*She puts her hand on his arm, and they go together towards the door in front of the staircase.*)

MISS FARRINGDON. Poor Gerald!

GERALD (*laughing*). Why poor? [*They go out together.*

The door on the right at the back opens quietly and BOB *comes in. He stands there for a moment looking at the hall, and then speaks over his shoulder to somebody behind him.*

BOB. It's all right, there's nobody here.

PAMELA. I wonder where Gerald is.

BOB. You're sure he's down here?

PAMELA. Yes, I had a letter from him; he told me he was going to be.

BOB (*going up to her*). Pamela, you can't see him alone.

PAMELA. I must; You can see him afterwards, but I must see him alone first.   Poor Gerald!

BOB. He never really loved you.

PAMELA. I don't think he did really, but it will hurt him.

BOB (*eagerly*). Say you're not sorry for what you're doing.

PAMELA. Aren't I doing it?

BOB. Say you love *me* and not Gerald.   Say you really love me, and it's not just because you are sorry for me.

PAMELA. Oh, I have so much in my heart for you, Bob. I'm glad I'm marrying you.   But you must always love me, and want me as you want me now.

BOB (*seizing her in his arms*). By God! you'll get that. (*He kisses her fiercely.*)

PAMELA (*satisfied*). Oh, Bob!   Oh, Bob!   I'm glad I found you at last.

> (*She goes away from him and stands looking into the fire, one hand on the mantelpiece.*)

BOB. Shall I go and look for Gerald?

PAMELA (*looking into the fire*). Yes.   No.   He'll come.

BOB. You won't let him talk you round?

PAMELA (*looking up at him in surprise*). Oh no; I'm quite safe now.

BOB. I can never thank you for all you've done, for all you've been to me.   When we are out of this cursèd country, and I have you to myself, I will try to show you. (*She says nothing, and he walks restlessly about the room.   He picks up a hat and says*) Hullo, Tommy's here.

PAMELA (*quickly*). I don't want to see him, I don't want to see anybody.   We must just tell Gerald and then go.

BOB. Anybody might come at any moment.   You

should have let me write as I wanted to. Or waited till he came back to London.

PAMELA. We've given up being cowards. Perhaps you'd better try and find him. We'll only tell Gerald. If we see the others, we'll just have to make the best of it.

BOB (*moving off towards the door in front of the staircase*). All right. If I find him I'll send him in here.

[*He goes out.*

(PAMELA *drops into a chair and remains looking at the fire.* GERALD, *coming down from the gallery above, suddenly catches sight of her.*)

GERALD (*rushing down the stairs*). Pamela! Why, Pamela! (*Excitedly*) Why are you—— You said to-morrow. Pamela, you said—— Never mind, you're here. Oh, bless you! (PAMELA *has got up to meet him, and he is now standing holding her hands, and looking at her happily.*) Pamela's here; all's right with the world. (*He leans forward to kiss her, but she stops him.*)

PAMELA (*nervously*). No, no; I've something to tell you, Gerald.

GERALD. I've got a thousand things to tell *you.*

PAMELA. Bob's here.

GERALD (*excited*). Bob? Did you come down with him?

PAMELA. Yes.

GERALD. I had a telegram, but it didn't say—— Did you meet him? Why didn't he tell us? Where is he?

PAMELA. He just went to look for you.

GERALD. I'll soon find him.

(*He turns away to go after* BOB, *but* PAMELA *stops him.*)

PAMELA. Gerald!

GERALD (*turning round*). Yes.

PAMELA. Never mind Bob for the moment. I wanted to see you alone.

GERALD (*coming back quickly*). Of course. Hang Bob! Come on the sofa and tell me everything. Jove! it's wonderful to see you again; you've been away for years.

> (*He takes her hand and tries to lead her towards the sofa, but she stops.*)

PAMELA. Gerald, you're making it very hard for me : I've got something to tell you.

GERALD (*afraid suddenly and speaking sharply*). What do you mean?

PAMELA. Oh, don't look at me like that—I know it will hurt you, but it won't be more than that. I want you to release me from my promise.

GERALD. What promise?

PAMELA (*in a low voice*). My promise to marry you.

GERALD. I don't understand. Why?

PAMELA (*bravely*). I want to marry Bob.

> (*Keeping his eyes on her all the time,* GERALD *moves slowly away from her.*)

GERALD (*to himself*). Bob! Bob! But you knew Bob first.

PAMELA. Yes.

GERALD. And then you promised to marry *me*. You couldn't have been in love with him. I don't understand.

PAMELA (*sadly*). I don't understand either, but that's how it's happened.

GERALD. And to think how I've been throwing you in Bob's way, and wanting you and him to be fond of each other. (*Fiercely*) *That* didn't make you think that I didn't love you?

PAMELA (*faltering*). I—I don't—you didn't——

GERALD. I was so confident of you. That was your fault. You made me.

PAMELA. I think you could have made me love you if you hadn't been so confident.

GERALD. I trusted you. You had told me. *I* knew I should never change, and I thought I knew *you* wouldn't.

PAMELA. I was wrong. I never did love you.

GERALD. Then why did you say——

PAMELA (*looking at him rather wistfully*). You're rather charming, Gerald, you know, and you——

GERALD (*turning away from her furiously*). Damn charming! That's what you all say. I'm sick of it! You think that if a man's charming, that's the end of him, and that all he's good for is to amuse a few old ladies at a tea-party. I'm sick of it! The rude rough man with the heart of gold—that's the only sort that can have a heart at all, according to some of you.

PAMELA (*utterly surprised by this*). Gerald!

GERALD. I'm sorry, Pamela. Of course you wouldn't understand. But we were just talking. (*With a sudden disarming smile*) I don't know whether an apology is overdoing the charm?

PAMELA (*in distress*). Oh, Gerald, you couldn't really have loved me; you don't really now. Of course, it will hurt you, but you'll soon get over it. Oh, what's the good of my talking like this? I've never really known you; I don't know you now.

GERALD (*quietly*). It's no good now, anyway. (*He walks away from her and looks out through the windows at the back.*) Just tell me one or two things. Were you in love with him when he went to prison?

PAMELA. I don't know really I don't know. I was so dreadfully sorry for him all that time before, and I felt so very friendly towards him, so very—oh, Gerald, so motherly. And I wanted to be wanted so badly, and you didn't seem to want me in that way. That was why, when he had gone, I went right away from you, and asked you not to write to me; I wanted to think it all out—alone.

GERALD. But you wrote to Bob?

PAMELA. Oh, Gerald, he wanted it so badly.

GERALD. I'm sorry.

PAMELA. I wrote to him and he wrote to me. I met him when he came out—he told me when to come. I suppose I had decided by then; we came down here to tell you. I had to come at once.

GERALD. You do love him, Pamela? It isn't just pity?

PAMELA. I do, Gerald; I think I found that out this afternoon. (*Timidly*) Say you don't hate me very much.

GERALD. I wish to God I could. . . . What are you and Bob going to do?

PAMELA. Canada, as soon as we can. I've got friends there. We've a little money between us. Bob ought to have done it a long time ago. (*Coming up to him*) Just do one more nice thing for me before we go.

GERALD (*moving away from her on pretence of getting a cigarette*). What is it?

PAMELA. Bob will want to see you before he goes.

GERALD. I don't want to see him.

PAMELA. Ah, but you must.

GERALD. What have we got to say to each other?

PAMELA. I don't know, but I feel you must see him. Otherwise he'll think that he ran away from you.

GERALD (*with a shrug*). All right. You'll go back to London at once, I suppose?

PAMELA. Yes. We hired a car. We left it outside at the gates. We didn't want to see anybody but you, if possible.

GERALD. Father and mother are out. Aunt Harriet knows—oh, and Tommy and Letty—that Bob was coming to-day; nobody else. But I can make up something. We'll keep Tommy and Letty out of it for the moment. Of course, they'll all have to know in the end.

PAMELA. We'll write, of course.

GERALD. Yes. Tommy and Letty are engaged, by the way.

PAMELA. Oh! (*Understanding how he must feel about it*) Oh, Gerald! (*She makes a movement towards him, but he takes no notice.*) I'll send Bob to you; he's waiting outside, I expect. (*Timidly*) Good-bye, Gerald.

GERALD (*still with his back to her*). Good-bye, Pamela.

PAMELA. Won't you——

GERALD (*from the bottom of his heart*). Go away, go away! I can't bear the sound of your voice; I can't bear to look at you. Go away!

PAMELA. Oh, Gerald!   [*She goes out.*

(GERALD *looks up as she goes out, and then looks quickly down again. When* BOB *comes in he is still resting with his arm on the mantelpiece looking into the fire.*)

GERALD (*looking up*). Hullo.

BOB. Hullo. (*After a pause*) Is that all you've got to say?

GERALD. I've just seen Pamela.

BOB (*trying not to show his eagerness*). Well?

GERALD. Well—isn't that enough?

BOB. What do you mean?

GERALD (*bitterly*). Do you want me to fall on your neck, and say take her and be happy?

BOB. You never loved her.

GERALD. That's a lie, and anyhow we won't discuss it. She's going to marry you, and that's an end of it.

BOB (*very eagerly*). She *is* going to?

GERALD (*sharply*). Don't you know it?

BOB (*mumbling*). Yes, but she might—— Ah, you couldn't charm her away from me this time.

GERALD (*with an effort*). I don't know what you mean by "*this* time." I think we'd better leave Pamela out of it altogether. She's waiting for you outside. Last time I offered to shake hands with you, you had some fancied grievance against me, and you wouldn't ; now if there's any grievance between us, it's on *my* side. (*Holding out his hand*) Good-bye, Bob, and—quite honestly—good luck.

BOB (*ignoring the hand*). Magnanimous Gerald !

> (GERALD *looks at him in surprise for a moment.
> Then he shrugs his shoulders, turns round, and
> goes back to the mantelpiece, and takes a
> cigarette from the box there.*)

GERALD. I'm tired of you, Bob. If you don't want me, I don't want you. (*He sits down in a chair and lights his cigarette.*)

BOB. And now I suppose you're thoroughly pleased with yourself, and quite happy.

GERALD (*looking at him in absolute wonder*). Happy ? You *fool !* (*Something in* BOB'*s face surprises him, and he gets up and says*) Why do you suddenly hate me like this ?

BOB (*with a bitter laugh*). Suddenly !

GERALD (*almost frightened*). Bob !

BOB (*letting the jealousy that has been pent up for years come out at last*). You're surprised ! Surprised ! You would be. You've never stopped to think what other people are thinking ; you take it for granted that they all love you, and that's all you care about. Do you think I liked playing second fiddle to you all my life ? Do you think I've never had any ambitions of my own ? I suppose you thought I was quite happy being one of the crowd of admirers round you, all saying, " Oh, look at Gerald, isn't he wonderful ?"

GERALD (*astounded*). Bob, I had no idea—I never dreamt——

BOB. They thought something of me when I was young. When I first went to school they thought something of me. I daresay even *you* thought something of me then; I could come back in the holidays and tell you what school was like, and what a lot they thought of me. They didn't think much of me when *you* came; you soon put a stop to that. I was just young Farringdon's brother then, and when we came home together, all the talk was of the wonderful things *Gerald* had done. It was like that at Eton; it was like that at Oxford. It's always been like that. I managed to get away from you a bit after Oxford, but it went on just the same. "How do you do, Mr. Farringdon? Are you any relation to Gerald Farringdon?" (*With the utmost contempt*) And you actually thought I liked that; you thought I enjoyed it. You thought I smiled modestly and said, "Oh yes, he's my brother, my young brother; isn't he wonderful?"

GERALD (*hardly able to realize it*). And you've felt like this for years? (*To himself*) For years!

BOB (*not noticing him*). And that wasn't enough for you. They got you into the Foreign Office—they could have got me there. They could have put me into the Army—— (*Almost shouting*) Aren't I the eldest son? But no, it didn't matter about the eldest son—never mind about him; put him in the City, anywhere as long as he's out of the way. If we have any influence, we must use it for Gerald—the wonderful Gerald.

GERALD. If this is an indictment, it's drawn against the wrong person.

BOB (*more quietly*). Then at last I found a friend; somebody who took me for my own sake. (*Bitterly*) And like a damned fool I brought her down here, and she saw *you*. I might have known what would happen.

GERALD. Pamela!

BOB. Yes, and you took her. After taking everything you could all your life, you took *her*. She was Bob's friend—that was quite enough. She must be one more in the crowd of admirers round you. So you took her. (*Triumphantly*) Ah, but I got her back in the end. I've got her now—and I think I'm square, Gerald.

GERALD. Yes, I think you're square now.

BOB (*rather jauntily, as he leans back against the end of the sofa and feels for his cigarette-case*). I seem to have surprised you rather.

GERALD. You've thought like that about me for years and you've never said anything? You've felt like that about Pamela and you've never said anything?

BOB. I've been thinking it over, particularly these last few months—in prison, Gerald. You have a lot of time for thinking in prison. Oh, I know; you advised me to stand on my head and waggle my legs in the air —something like that. You were full of brilliant ideas. I had a better idea—I *thought*.

GERALD (*realizing his state of mind*). My God, what a time you must have had!

BOB (*furiously*). Damn you! I *won't* be pitied by you.

GERALD (*coolly*). And you're not going to be. You've talked about yourself and thought about yourself quite long enough; now I'm going to talk about *my*self.

BOB. And it won't be the first time either.

GERALD (*quickly*). It will be the first time to *you*. You say I've never tried to understand your feelings— have you ever tried to understand mine? My God, Bob! I've thought a good deal more about you than you have about me. Have I ever talked about myself to you? When a boy does well at school he likes talk-

ing about it; did I ever bore *you* with it? Never!
Because I knew how you'd feel about it. I knew
how *I'd* feel about it, and so I tried to make it easy
for *you*.

BOB. Very noble of you.

GERALD (*angrily*). Don't be such a damned fool, Bob
What's the good of talking like that? If whatever I
do is wrong, then you're only convicting yourself;
you're not convicting me. According to you, if I talk
about myself I'm being conceited and superior, and if I
don't talk about myself, I'm being noble and still more
superior. In fact, whatever I do, I can't please you.
That doesn't condemn me; it condemns yourself.
(*Wearily*) What's the good of talking?

BOB. Go on; I like to hear it.

GERALD. Very well. We'll take the definite accusa-
tions first. Apart from the general charge of being
successful—whatever that amounts to—you accuse me
of two things. One you didn't mention just now, but it
was more or less obvious the last time I saw you. That
was that I neglected to help you when you were in
trouble, and that through me you went to prison.

BOB. Yes, I forgot that this time. (*With an unpleasant
laugh*) But I didn't forget it in prison.

GERALD. You had a sense of humour once, Bob. I
don't know what's happened to it lately. Don't you
think it's rather funny to hate a person steadily for
fifteen years, judge all his acts as you'd hardly judge
those of your bitterest enemy, and yet, the first time
you are in trouble, to expect him to throw everything
on one side and rush to your help—and then to feel
bitterly ill-used if he doesn't?

BOB (*rather taken aback*). I—you didn't—I didn't——

GERALD (*quietly*). That's been rather like you all
through, Bob. You were always the one who had to be

helped ; you were always the one who was allowed to
have the grievance. Still, that doesn't make it any
better for me if I could have helped you and didn't.
However, I'm quite certain that I *couldn't* have helped
you then. We'll take the other accusation, that I stole
Pamela from you. I've only got two things to say to
that. First, that Pamela was not engaged to you, and
was perfectly free to choose between us. Secondly,
that you never told me, and I hadn't the slightest idea,
that you were the least bit fond of her. Indeed, I
don't believe you realized it yourself at that time.

BOB (*rather shamefaced*). I've realized it since.

GERALD. Yes, and you've taken Pamela back since. I
think if I were you I would keep her out of it. (BOB
looks away and GERALD *goes on*) Now we come to the
general charge, which seems to be (*very deliberately*) that
I'm better than you at games, that I've got better
manners than you, that I'm cleverer than you—in fact,
that I'm superior to you in every outward way, and am
only inferior to you in—well, in the moral qualities.
(*Quietly*) Bob, what are these moral qualities in which I
am so deficient and you so endowed ? You judge me by
the qualities I am supposed to have shown to you ;
now what have you shown to *me* ? Have *you* been
generous, have *you* been friendly, have *you* been sympathetic ? No ; you've just told me that for fifteen years
you've hated me and been jealous of me. Things have
been rotten for you, I admit ; have you ever tried to
make the best of them ? You've had disadvantages to
fight against ; have you ever fought against them ?
Never ! You've turned every trouble into a grievance,
and hoarded it up. I said just now I was sick of you. I
am—utterly. You said just now you didn't want my
pity. You haven't got it ; you've only got my contempt.
. . . (*He turns away, and then suddenly turns back, and,*

holding out his hand to BOB, *says utterly unexpectedly*) And *now,* damn you ! will you shake hands ?

BOB (*incoherent with surprise*). What do you—I—you didn't—— (GERALD'S *hand is still held out, and he is smiling.*) Oh, Jerry ! (*He takes the hand.*)

GERALD. That's all right. Good-bye, Bob, and good luck.

BOB (*bewildered*). Good-bye. (*He turns round and goes towards the door. Half-way there, he looks over his shoulder and says awkwardly*) Had rather a rotten time in prison. (GERALD *nods. At the door* BOB *says*) Pamela and I——

> [*With rather a forced smile,* GERALD *nods again, and* BOB *goes out.*

> (*Left alone,* GERALD *stands looking into the fire and thinking. He tries sitting down to see if that will make thinking any pleasanter ; then he tries standing up again. He goes to the door in front of the staircase and opens it to see if there is anybody there ; then he goes to the windows at the back and looks through them. Evidently he sees somebody, for he beckons and then returns to his old place by the fire. In a few moments* LETTY *and* TOMMY *come in.*)

TOMMY (*excitedly*). I say, has Bob come ?

GERALD. Why ?

TOMMY. I could have sworn we saw him just now as we were coming in. At least, Letty swore she did——

LETTY. I *know* I did.

TOMMY. So I gave him a shout, but he fairly trekked off. Was it Bob ?

GERALD. Yes. Now look here, I want you to be two nice people. Don't say anything to anybody. He came, but he didn't want to see the whole crowd of us. He's going to Canada. I'll do all the explaining, if you two just say nothing. Do you see ?

LETTY. Of course, Gerald.

TOMMY. Rather, old boy. Besides, it will make it much better for Letty and me.

LETTY. No rival attraction, Tommy means.

Enter SIR JAMES *and* LADY FARRINGDON *from the outer hall, having just returned from their lunch.*

SIR JAMES. Ah! here you all are.

GERALD. Had a good lunch?

SIR JAMES. Lunch was all right, but the people were dull, very dull.

LADY FARRINGDON. There vere one or two nice ones, I thought, dear. They all knew about *you*, Gerald.

TOMMY (*proudly*). Of course they would.

SIR JAMES. Oh, one or two were all right, but *he* was —well, I was discussing shorthorns with him after lunch, and he hardly seemed interested at all. Dull, very dull. I've got no use for that sort of man.

(*During this speech the Butler has come in with a telegram for* GERALD.)

GERALD (*taking it*). Just a moment. (*He reads it quickly.*) No answer.   [*Exit Butler.*

(GERALD *reads his telegram again more thoughtfully.*)

LADY FARRINGDON. From Pamela, dear?

GERALD. From the office. I shall have to go up at once.

LADY FARRINGDON (*very disappointed*). Oh, Gerald!

SIR JAMES. Something on?

GERALD. Rather an important thing really. I never thought I should get it, but there was just a chance. (*Looking at his watch*) Oh, I can do it comfortably.

SIR JAMES (*obviously proud that* GERALD *is in the thick of things*). What is it? I suppose you mustn't tell us.

GERALD. Something abroad.

SIR JAMES. Diplomatic mission, eh?

GERALD. Yes.

LETTY. That does sound so frightfully exciting.

LADY FARRINGDON (*proudly*). Oh, Gerald! (*Thoughtfully*). I wish we had known about it this morning, we could have mentioned it at lunch.

SIR JAMES. That ought to lead to something.

GERALD. Yes. I think it will. It's rather an opportunity.

> (*They are all round him now, just as they have always been. The buzz begins.*)

SIR JAMES. Aha! you'll be an ambassador yet. What do you think of that, Letty?

LETTY. Well done, Gerald.

LADY FARRINGDON. How like you, Gerald!

TOMMY. Good old Gerald! I never knew such a chap. You really *are!*

GERALD (*softly*). I wish I weren't, Tommy! Oh, I wish I weren't!

> (*They don't hear him; they are still buzzing.*)

THE BOY COMES HOME

A COMEDY IN ONE ACT

CHARACTERS.

UNCLE JAMES.
AUNT EMILY.
PHILIP.
MARY.
MRS. HIGGINS.

THIS play was first produced by Mr. Owen Nares at the Victoria Palace Theatre on September 9, 1918, with the following cast:

Philip -	-	OWEN NARES.
Uncle James -		TOM REYNOLDS.
Aunt Emily	-	DOROTHY RADFORD.
Mary -	-	ADAH DICK.
Mrs. Higgins -		RACHEL DE SOLLA.

THE BOY COMES HOME

SCENE.—*A room in* UNCLE JAMES'S *house in the Cromwell Road.*

TIME.—*The day after the War.*

Any room in UNCLE JAMES'S *house is furnished in heavy mid-Victorian style ; this particular morning-room is perhaps solider and more respectable even than the others, from the heavy table in the middle of it to the heavy engravings on the walls. There are two doors to it. The one at the back opens into the hall, the one at the side into the dining-room.*

PHILIP *comes in from the hall and goes into the dining-room. Apparently he finds nothing there, for he returns to the morning-room, looks about him for a moment and then rings the bell. It is ten o'clock, and he wants his breakfast. He picks up the paper, and sits in a heavy armchair in front of the fire—a pleasant-looking well-built person of twenty-three, with an air of decisiveness about him.* MARY, *the parlour-maid, comes in.*

MARY. Did you ring, Master Philip ?

PHILIP (*absently*). Yes ; I want some breakfast, please, Mary.

MARY (*coldly*). Breakfast has been cleared away an hour ago.

PHILIP. Exactly. That's why I rang. You can boil me a couple of eggs or something. And coffee, not tea.

MARY. I am sure I don't know what Mrs. Higgins will say?

PHILIP (*getting up*). Who is Mrs. Higgins?

MARY. The cook. And she's not used to being put about like this.

PHILIP. Do you think she'll say something?

MARY. I don't know *what* she'll say.

PHILIP. You needn't tell me, you know, if you don't want to. Anyway, I don't suppose it will shock me. One gets used to it in the Army. (*He smiles pleasantly at her.*)

MARY. Well, I'll do what I can, sir. But breakfast at eight sharp is the master's rule, just as it used to be before you went away to the war.

PHILIP. Before I went away to the war I did a lot of silly things. Don't drag them up now. (*More curtly*) Two eggs, and if there's a ham bring that along too. (*He turns away.*)

MARY (*doubtfully, as she prepares to go*). Well, I'm sure I don't know what Mrs. Higgins will say. [*Exit Mary.*
        (*As she goes out she makes way for* AUNT EMILY *to
            come in, a kind-hearted mid-Victorian lady who
            has never had any desire for the vote.*)

EMILY. *There* you are, Philip! Good-morning, dear. Did you sleep well?

PHILIP. Rather; splendidly, thanks, Aunt Emily. How are you? (*He kisses her.*)

EMILY. And did you have a good breakfast? Naughty boy to be late for it. I always thought they had to get up so early in the Army.

PHILIP. They do. That's why they're so late when they get out of the Army.

EMILY. Dear me! I should have thought a habit of four years would have stayed with you.

PHILIP. Every morning for four years, as I've shot

out of bed, I've said to myself, "Wait! A time will come." (*Smiling*) That doesn't really give a habit a chance.

EMILY. Well, I daresay you wanted your sleep out. I was so afraid that a really cosy bed would keep you awake after all those years in the trenches.

PHILIP. Well, one isn't in the trenches all the time. And one gets leave—if one's an officer.

EMILY (*reproachfully*). You didn't spend much of it with *us*, Philip.

PHILIP (*taking her hands*). I know; but you did understand, didn't you, dear?

EMILY. We're not very gay, and I know you must have wanted gaiety for the little time you had. But I think your Uncle James felt it. After all, dear, you've lived with us for some years, and he *is* your guardian.

PHILIP. I know. *You've* been a darling to me always, Aunt Emily. But (*awkwardly*) Uncle James and I——

EMILY. Of course, he is a *little* difficult to get on with. I'm more used to him. But I'm sure he really is very fond of you, Philip.

PHILIP. H'm! I always used to be frightened of him. . . . I suppose he's just the same. He seemed just the same last night—and he still has breakfast at eight o'clock. Been making pots of money, I suppose?

EMILY. He never tells me exactly, but he did speak once about the absurdity of the excess-profits tax. You see, jam is a thing the Army wants.

PHILIP. It certainly gets it.

EMILY. It was so nice for him, because it made him feel he was doing his bit, helping the poor men in the trenches.

Enter MARY.

MARY. Mrs. Higgins wishes to speak to you, ma'am. (*She looks at* PHILIP *as much as to say,* " *There you are !*")

EMILY (*getting up*). Yes, I'll come.   (*To* PHILIP) I think I'd better just see what she wants, Philip.

PHILIP (*firmly to* MARY). Tell Mrs. Higgins to come here. (MARY *hesitates and looks at her mistress.*) At once, please.   [*Exit* MARY.

EMILY (*upset*). Philip, dear, I don't know what Mrs. Higgins will say——

PHILIP. No ; nobody seems to.   I thought we might really find out for once.

EMILY (*going towards the door*). Perhaps I'd better go——

PHILIP (*putting his arm round her waist*). Oh no, you mustn't.   You see, she really wants to see *me*.

EMILY. *You ?*

PHILIP. Yes ; I ordered breakfast five minutes ago.

EMILY. Philip !   My poor boy !   Why didn't you tell me ? and I daresay I could have got it for you.   Though I don't know what Mrs. Higgins——

(*An extremely angry voice is heard outside, and* MRS. HIGGINS, *stout and aggressive, comes in.*)

MRS. HIGGINS (*truculently*). You sent for me, ma'am ?

EMILY (*nervously*). Yes—er—I think if you—per- haps——

PHILIP (*calmly*). *I* sent for you, Mrs. Higgins.   I want some breakfast.   Didn't Mary tell you ?

MRS. HIGGINS. Breakfast is at eight o'clock.   It always has been as long as I've been in this house, and always will be until I get further orders.

PHILIP. Well, you've just got further orders.   Two eggs, and if there's a ham——

MRS. HIGGINS. Orders.   We're talking about orders.

From whom in this house do I take orders, may I ask?

PHILIP. In this case from me.

MRS. HIGGINS (*playing her trump-card*). In that case, ma'am, I wish to give a month's notice from to-day. *In*clusive.

PHILIP (*quickly, before his aunt can say anything*). Certainly. In fact, you'd probably prefer it if my aunt gave *you* notice, and then you could go at once. We can easily arrange that. (*To* AUNT EMILY *as he takes out a fountain-pen and cheque-book*) What do you pay her?

EMILY (*faintly*). Forty-five pounds.

PHILIP (*writing on his knee*). Twelves into forty-five. . . . (*Pleasantly to* MRS. HIGGINS, *but without looking up*) I hope you don't mind a Cox's cheque. Some people do; but this is quite a good one. (*Tearing it out*) Here you are.

MRS. HIGGINS (*taken aback*). What's this?

PHILIP. Your wages instead of notice. Now you can go at once.

MRS. HIGGINS. Who said anything about going?

PHILIP (*surprised*). I'm sorry; I thought *you* did.

MRS. HIGGINS. If it's only a bit of breakfast, I don't say but what I mightn't get it, if I'm asked decent.

PHILIP (*putting back the cheque*). Then let me say again, "Two eggs, ham and coffee." And Mary can bring the ham up at once, and I'll get going on that. (*Turning away*) Thanks very much.

MRS. HIGGINS. Well, I—well—well! [*Exit speechless.*

PHILIP (*surprised*). Is that all she ever says? It isn't much to worry about.

EMILY. Philip, how could you! I should have been terrified.

PHILIP. Well, you see, I've done your job for two years out there.

EMILY. What job?

PHILIP. Mess President. . . . I think I'll go and see about that ham.

> (*He smiles at her and goes out into the dining-room.* AUNT EMILY *wanders round the room, putting a few things tidy as is her habit, when she is interrupted by the entrance of* UNCLE JAMES. JAMES *is not a big man, nor an impressive one in his black morning-coat; and his thin straggly beard, now going grey, does not hide a chin of any great power; but he has a severity which passes for strength with the weak.*)

JAMES. Philip down yet?

EMILY. He's just having his breakfast.

JAMES (*looking at his watch*). Ten o'clock. (*Snapping it shut and putting it back*) Ten o'clock. I say ten o'clock, Emily.

EMILY. Yes, dear, I heard you.

JAMES. You don't say anything?

EMILY (*vaguely*). I expect he's tired after that long war.

JAMES. That's no excuse for not being punctual. I suppose he learnt punctuality in the Army?

EMILY. I expect he learnt it, James, but I understood him to say that he'd forgotten it.

JAMES. Then the sooner he learns it again the better. I particularly stayed away from the office to-day in order to talk things over with him, and (*looking at his watch*) here's ten o'clock—past ten—and no sign of him. I'm practically throwing away a day.

EMILY. What are you going to talk to him about?

JAMES. His future, naturally. I have decided that the best thing he can do is to come into the business at once.

EMILY. Are you really going to talk it over with him,

James, or are you just going to tell him that he *must* come?

JAMES (*surprised*). What do you mean? What's the difference? Naturally we shall talk it over first, and—er—naturally he'll fall in with my wishes.

EMILY. I suppose he can hardly help himself, poor boy.

JAMES. Not until he's twenty-five, anyhow. When he's twenty-five he can have his own money and do what he likes with it.

EMILY (*timidly*). But I think you ought to consult him a little, dear. After all, he *has* been fighting for us.

JAMES (*with his back to the fire*). Now that's the sort of silly sentiment that there's been much too much of. I object to it strongly. I don't want to boast, but I think I may claim to have done my share. I gave up my nephew to my country, and I—er—suffered from the shortage of potatoes to an extent that you probably didn't realize Indeed, if it hadn't been for your fortunate discovery about that time that you didn't really like potatoes, I don't know how we should have carried on. And, as I think I've told you before, the excess-profits tax seemed to me a singularly stupid piece of legislation—but I paid it. And I don't go boasting about how much I paid.

EMILY (*unconvinced*). Well, I think that Philip's four years out there have made him more of a man; he doesn't seem somehow like a boy who can be told what to do. I'm sure they've taught him something.

JAMES. I've no doubt that they've taught him something about—er—bombs and—er—which end a revolver goes off, and how to form fours. But I don't see that that sort of thing helps him to decide upon the most suitable career for a young man in after-war conditions.

EMILY. Well, I can only say you'll find him different

JAMES. I didn't notice any particular difference last night.

EMILY. I think you'll find him rather more—I can't quite think of the word, but Mrs. Higgins could tell you what I mean.

JAMES. Of course, if he likes to earn his living any other way, he may; but I don t see how he proposes to do it so long as I hold the purse-strings. (*Looking at his watch*) Perhaps you'd better tell him that I cannot wait any longer.

(EMILY *opens the door leading into the dining-room and talks through it to* PHILIP.)

EMILY. Philip, your uncle is waiting to see you before he goes to the office. Will you be long, dear?

PHILIP (*from the dining-room*). Is he in a hurry?

JAMES (*shortly*). Yes.

EMILY. He says he *is* rather, dear.

PHILIP. Couldn't he come and talk in here? It wouldn't interfere with my breakfast.

JAMES. No.

EMILY. He says he'd rather you came to *him*, darling.

PHILIP (*resigned*). Oh, well.

EMILY (*to* JAMES). He'll be here directly, dear. Just sit down in front of the fire and make yourself comfortable with the paper. He won't keep you long. (*She arranges him.*)

JAMES (*taking the paper*). The morning is not the time to make oneself comfortable. It's a most dangerous habit. I nearly found myself dropping off in front of the fire just now. I don't like this hanging about, wasting the day. (*He opens the paper.*)

EMILY. You should have had a nice sleep, dear, while you could. We were up so late last night listening to Philip's stories.

JAMES. Yes, yes. (*He begins a yawn and stifles it*

hurriedly.) You mustn't neglect your duties, Emily. I've no doubt you have plenty to do.

EMILY. All right, James, then I'll leave you. But don't be hard on the boy.

JAMES (*sleepily*). I shall be just, Emily; you can rely upon that.

EMILY (*going to the door*). I don't think that's quite what I meant.   [*She goes out.*

(JAMES, *who is now quite comfortable, begins to nod. He wakes up with a start, turns over the paper, and nods again. Soon he is breathing deeply with closed eyes.*)

*   *   *   *

PHILIP (*coming in*). Sorry to have kept you waiting, but I was a bit late for breakfast. (*He takes out his pipe.*) Are we going to talk business or what?

JAMES (*taking out his watch*): A *bit* late! I make it just two hours.

PHILIP (*pleasantly*). All right, Uncle James. Call it two hours late. Or twenty-two hours early for to-morrow's breakfast, if you like. (*He sits down in a chair on the opposite side of the table from his uncle, and lights his pipe.*)

JAMES. You smoke now?

PHILIP (*staggered*). I what?

JAMES (*nodding at his pipe*). You smoke?

PHILIP. Good heavens! what did you think we *did* in France?

JAMES. Before you start smoking all over the house, I should have thought you would have asked your aunt's permission.

(PHILIP *looks at him in amazement, and then goes to the door.*)

PHILIP (*calling*). Aunt Emily! . . . Aunt Emily! . . . Do you mind my smoking in here?

AUNT EMILY (*from upstairs*). Of course not, darling.

PHILIP (*to* JAMES, *as he returns to his chair*). Of course not, darling. (*He puts back his pipe in his mouth.*)

JAMES. Now, understand once and for all, Philip, while you remain in my house I expect not only punctuality, but also civility and respect. I will *not* have impertinence.

PHILIP (*unimpressed*). Well, that's what I want to talk to you about, Uncle James. About staying in your house, I mean.

JAMES. I don't know what you do mean.

PHILIP. Well, we don't get on too well together, and I thought perhaps I'd better take rooms somewhere. You could give me an allowance until I came into my money. Or I suppose you could give me the money now if you really liked. I don't quite know how father left it to me.

JAMES (*coldly*). You come into your money when you are twenty-five. Your father very wisely felt that to trust a large sum to a mere boy of twenty-one was simply putting temptation in his way. Whether I have the power or not to alter his dispositions, I certainly don't propose to do so.

PHILIP. If it comes to that, I *am* twenty-five.

JAMES. Indeed ? I had an impression that that event took place in about two years' time. When did you become twenty-five, may I ask ?

PHILIP (*quietly*). It was on the Somme. We were attacking the next day and my company was in support. We were in a so-called trench on the edge of a wood— a damned rotten place to be, and we got hell. The company commander sent back to ask if we could move. The C.O. said, " Certainly not ; hang on." We hung on ; doing nothing, you know—just hanging on and waiting for the next day. Of course, the Boche knew all about that. He had it on us nicely. . . . (*Sadly*) Poor old Billy! he was one of the best—our company commander, you know. They got him, poor devil! That left *me* in command of the company. I sent a runner back to ask if I could move. Well, I'd had a bit of a scout on my own and found a sort of trench five hundred yards to the right. Not what *you'd* call a trench, of course, but compared to that wood—well, it was absolutely Hyde Park. I described the position and asked if I could go there. My man never came back. I waited an hour and sent another man. He went west too. Well, I wasn't going to send a third. It was murder. So I had to decide. We'd lost about half the company by this time, you see. Well, there were three things I could do—hang on, move to this other trench, against orders, or go back myself and explain the situation. . . . I moved. . . . And then I went back to the C.O. and told him I'd moved. . . . And then I went back to the company again. . . . (*Quietly*) That was when I became twenty-five. . . . or thirty-five. . . . or forty-five.

JAMES (*recovering himself with an effort*). Ah yes, yes. (*He coughs awkwardly.*) No doubt points like that frequently crop up in the trenches. I am glad that you did well out there, and I'm sure your Colonel would speak kindly of you; but when it comes to choosing a career for you now that you have left the Army, my advice is not altogether to be despised. Your father evidently thought so, or he would not have entrusted you to my care.

PHILIP. My father didn't foresee this war.

JAMES. Yes, yes, but you make too much of this war. All you young boys seem to think you've come back from France to teach us our business. You'll find that it is you who'll have to learn, not we.

PHILIP. I'm quite prepared to learn; in fact, I want to.

JAMES. Excellent. Then we can consider that settled.

PHILIP. Well, we haven't settled yet what business I'm going to learn.

JAMES. I don't think that's very difficult. I propose to take you into my business. You'll start at the bottom, of course, but it will be a splendid opening for you.

PHILIP (*thoughtfully*). I see. So you've decided it for me? The jam business.

JAMES (*sharply*). Is there anything to be ashamed of in that?

PHILIP. Oh no, nothing at all. Only it doesn't happen to appeal to me.

JAMES. If you knew which side your bread was buttered, it would appeal to you very considerably.

PHILIP. I'm afraid I can't see the butter for the jam.

JAMES. I don't want any silly jokes of that sort. You were glad enough to get it out there, I've no doubt.

PHILIP. Oh yes. Perhaps that's why I'm so sick of it now. . . . No, it's no good, Uncle James; you must think of something else.

JAMES (*with a sneer*). Perhaps *you've* thought of something else?

PHILIP. Well, I had some idea of being an architect——

JAMES. You propose to start learning to be an architect at twenty-three?

PHILIP (*smiling*). Well, I couldn't start before, could I?

JAMES. Exactly. And now you'll find it's too late.

PHILIP. Is it? Aren't there going to be any more architects, or doctors, or solicitors, or barristers? Because we've all lost four years of our lives, are all the professions going to die out?

JAMES. And how old do you suppose you'll be before you're earning money as an architect?

PHILIP. The usual time, whatever that may be. If I'm four years behind, so is everybody else.

JAMES. Well, I think it's high time you began to earn a living at once.

PHILIP. Look here, Uncle James, do you really think that you can treat me like a boy who's just left school? Do you think four years at the front have made no difference at all?

JAMES. If there had been any difference, I should have expected it to take the form of an increased readiness to obey orders and recognize authority.

PHILIP (*regretfully*). You are evidently determined to have a row. Perhaps I had better tell you once and for all that I refuse to go into the turnip and vegetable marrow business.

JAMES (*thumping the table angrily*). And perhaps I'd better tell *you*, sir, once and for all, that I don't propose to allow rude rudeness from an impertinent young puppy.

PHILIP (*reminiscently*). I remember annoying our Brigadier once. He was covered with red, had a very red face, about twenty medals, and a cold blue eye. He told me how angry he was for about five minutes while I stood to attention. I'm afraid you aren't nearly so impressive, Uncle James.

JAMES (*rather upset*). Oh! (*Recovering himself*) Fortunately I have other means of impressing you. The power of the purse goes a long way in this world. I propose to use it.

PHILIP. I see. . . . Yes . . . that's rather awkward, isn't it?

JAMES (*pleasantly*). I think you'll find it very awkward.

PHILIP (*thoughtfully*). Yes.

(*With an amused laugh* JAMES *settles down to his paper as if the interview were over.*)

9

PHILIP (*to himself*). I suppose I shall have to think of another argument. (*He takes out a revolver from his pocket and fondles it affectionately.*)

JAMES (*looking up suddenly as he is doing this—amazed*). What on earth are you doing?

PHILIP. Souvenir from France. Do you know, Uncle James, that this revolver has killed about twenty Germans?

JAMES (*shortly*). Oh! Well, don't go playing about with it here, or you'll be killing Englishmen before you know where you are.

PHILIP. Well, you never know. (*He raises it leisurely and points it at his uncle.*) It's a nice little weapon.

JAMES (*angrily*). Put it down, sir. You ought to have grown out of monkey tricks like that in the Army. You ought to know better than to point an unloaded revolver at anybody. That's the way accidents always happen.

PHILIP. Not when you've been on a revolver course and know all about it. Besides, it *is* loaded.

JAMES (*very angry because he is frightened suddenly*). Put it down at once, sir. (*PHILIP turns it away from him and examines it carelessly.*) What's the matter with you? Have you gone mad suddenly?

PHILIP (*mildly*). I thought you'd be interested in it. It's shot such a lot of Germans.

JAMES. Well, it won't want to shoot any more, and the sooner you get rid of it the better.

PHILIP. I wonder. Does it ever occur to you, Uncle James, that there are about a hundred thousand people in England who own revolvers, who are quite accustomed to them and—who have nobody to practise on now?

JAMES. No, sir, it certainly doesn't.

PHILIP (*thoughtfully*). I wonder if it will make any difference. You know, one gets so used to potting at people. It's rather difficult to realize suddenly that one oughtn't to.

JAMES (*getting up*). I don't know what the object of all this tomfoolery is, if it has one. But you understand that I expect you to come to the office with me to-morrow at nine o'clock. Kindly see that you're punctual. (*He turns to go away.*)

PHILIP (*softly*). Uncle James.

JAMES (*over his shoulder*). I have no more——

PHILIP (*in his parade voice*). Damn it, sir! stand to attention when you talk to an officer ! (JAMES *instinctively turns round and stiffens himself.*) That's better ; you can sit down if you like. (*He motions* JAMES *to his chair with the revolver.*)

JAMES (*going nervously to his chair*). What does this bluff mean ?

PHILIP. It isn't bluff, it's quite serious. (*Pointing the revolver at his uncle*) Do sit down.

JAMES (*sitting down*). Threats, eh ?

PHILIP. Persuasion.

JAMES. At the point of the revolver? You settle your arguments by force? Good heavens, sir ! this is just the very thing that we were fighting to put down.

PHILIP. *We* were fighting ! *We ! We !* Uncle, you're a humorist.

JAMES. Well, "you," if you prefer it. Although those of us who stayed at home——

PHILIP. Yes, never mind about the excess profits now. I can tell you quite well what we fought for. We used force to put down force. That's what I'm doing now. You were going to use force—the force of money—to make me do what you wanted. Now I'm using force to stop it (*He levels the revolver again.*)

JAMES. You're—you're going to shoot your old uncle ?

PHILIP. Why not? I've shot lots of old uncles—Landsturmers.

JAMES. But those were Germans! It's different shooting Germans. You're in England now. You couldn't have a crime on your conscience like that.

PHILIP. Ah, but you mustn't think that after four years of war one has quite the same ideas about the sanctity of human life. How could one?

JAMES. You'll find that juries have kept pretty much the same ideas, I fancy.

PHILIP. Yes, but revolvers often go off accidentally. You said so yourself. This is going to be the purest accident. Can't you see it in the papers? "The deceased's nephew, who was obviously upset——"

JAMES. I suppose you think it's brave to come back from the front and threaten a defenceless man with a revolver? Is that the sort of fair play they teach you in the Army?

PHILIP. Good heavens! of course it is. You don't think that you wait until the other side has got just as many guns as you before you attack? You're really rather lucky. Strictly speaking, I ought to have thrown half a dozen bombs at you first. (*Taking one out of his pocket*) As it happens, I've only got one.

JAMES (*thoroughly alarmed*). Put that back at once.

PHILIP (*putting down the revolver and taking it in his hands*). You hold it in the right hand—so—taking care to keep the lever down. Then you take the pin in the finger—so, and—but perhaps this doesn't interest you?

JAMES (*edging his chair away*). Put it down at once, sir. Good heavens! anything might happen.

PHILIP (*putting it down and taking up the revolver again*). Does it ever occur to you, Uncle James, that there are about three million people in England who know all about bombs, and how to throw them, and——

JAMES. It certainly does not occur to me.   I should never dream of letting these things occur to me.

PHILIP (*looking at the bomb regretfully*). It's rather against my principles as a soldier, but just to make things a bit more fair—(*generously*) you shall have it. (*He holds it out to him suddenly.*)

JAMES (*shrinking back again*). Certainly not, sir.   It might go off at any moment.

PHILIP (*putting it back in his pocket*). Oh no ; it's quite useless ; there's no detonator. . . .   (*Sternly*) Now, then, let's talk business.

JAMES. What do you want me to do ?

PHILIP. Strictly speaking, you should be holding your hands over your head and saying " Kamerad !"   However, I'll let you off that.   All I ask from you is that you should be reasonable.

JAMES. And if I refuse, you'll shoot me ?

PHILIP. Well, I don't quite know, Uncle James   I expect we should go through this little scene again to-morrow.   You haven't enjoyed it, have you ?   Well, there's lots more of it to come.   We'll rehearse it every day.   One day, if you go on being unreasonable, the thing will go off.   Of course, you think that I shouldn't have the pluck to fire.   But you can't be quite certain. It's a hundred to one that I shan't—only I might. Fear—it's a horrible thing.   Elderly men die of it sometimes.

JAMES. Pooh ! I'm not to be bluffed like that.

PHILIP (*suddenly*). You're quite right ; you're not that sort.   I made a mistake.   (*Aiming carefully*) I shall have to do it straight off, after all.   One—two——

JAMES (*on his knees, with uplifted hands, in an agony of terror*). Philip !   Mercy !   What are your terms ?

PHILIP (*picking him up by the scruff, and helping him into the chair*). Good man, that's the way to talk.   I'll get them for you.   Make yourself comfortable in front of the fire till I come back.   Here's the paper.   (*He gives his uncle the paper, and goes out into the hall.*)

*   *   *   *   *

> (JAMES *opens his eyes with a start and looks round him in a bewildered way.   He rubs his head, takes out his watch and looks at it, and then stares round the room again.   The door from the dining-room opens, and* PHILIP *comes in with a piece of toast in his hand.*)

PHILIP (*his mouth full*). You wanted to see me, Uncle James ?

JAMES (*still bewildered*). That's all right, my boy, that's all right.   What have you been doing ?

PHILIP (*surprised*). Breakfast.   (*Putting the last piece in his mouth*) Rather late, I'm afraid.

JAMES. That's all right.   (*He laughs awkwardly.*)

PHILIP. Anything the matter ?   You don't look your usual bright self.

JAMES. I—er—seem to have dropped asleep in front of the fire.   Most unusual thing for me to have done.   Most unusual.

PHILIP. Let that be a lesson to you not to get up so early.   Of course, if you're in the Army you can't help yourself.   Thank Heaven I'm out of it, and my own master again.

JAMES. Ah, that's what I wanted to talk to you about.   Sit down, Philip.   (*He indicates the chair by the fire.*)

PHILIP (*taking a chair by the table*). You have that, uncle ; I shall be all right here.

JAMES (*hastily*). No, no ; you come here.   (*He gives* PHILIP *the armchair and sits by the table himself.*)   I should be dropping off again.   (*He laughs awkwardly.*)

PHILIP. Righto.   (*He puts his hand to his pocket.* UNCLE JAMES *shivers and looks at him in horror.* PHILIP

brings out his pipe, and a sickly grin of relief comes into
JAMES's *face.*)

JAMES. I suppose you smoked a lot in France?

PHILIP. Rather! Nothing else to do. It's allowed
in here?

JAMES (*hastily*). Yes, yes, of course. (PHILIP *lights his
pipe.*) Well now, Philip, what are you going to do, now
you've left the Army?

PHILIP (*promptly*). Burn my uniform and sell my
revolver.

JAMES (*starting at the word "revolver"*). Sell your
revolver, eh?

PHILIP (*surprised*). Well, I don't want it now, do I?

JAMES. No. . . . Oh no. . . . Oh, most certainly
not, I should say. Oh, I can't see why you should
want it at all. (*With an uneasy laugh*) You're in England
now. No need for revolvers here—eh?

PHILIP (*staring at him*). Well, no, I hope not.

JAMES (*hastily*). Quite so. Well now, Philip, what
next? We must find a profession for you.

PHILIP (*yawning*). I suppose so. I haven't really
thought about it much.

JAMES. You never wanted to be an architect?

PHILIP (*surprised*). Architect? (JAMES *rubs his head
and wonders what made him think of architect.*)

JAMES. Or anything like that.

PHILIP. It's a bit late, isn't it?

JAMES. Well, if you're four years behind, so is everybody else. (*He feels vaguely that he has heard this
argument before.*)

PHILIP (*smiling*). To tell the truth, I don't feel I
mind much anyway. Anything you like—except a
commissionaire. I absolutely refuse to wear uniform
again.

JAMES. How would you like to come into the business?

PHILIP. The jam business? Well, I don't know. You wouldn't want me to salute you in the mornings?

JAMES. My dear boy, no!

PHILIP. All right, I'll try it if you like. I don't know if I shall be any good—what do you do?

JAMES. It's your experience in managing and—er—handling men which I hope will be of value.

PHILIP. Oh, I can do that all right. (*Stretching himself luxuriously*) Uncle James, do you realize that I'm never going to salute again, or wear a uniform, or get wet—really wet, I mean—or examine men's feet, or stand to attention when I'm spoken to, or—oh, lots more things. And best of all, I'm never going to be frightened again. Have you ever known what it is to be afraid—really afraid?

JAMES (*embarrassed*). I—er—well—— (*He coughs.*)

PHILIP. No, you couldn't—not really afraid of death, I mean. Well, that's over now. Good lord! I could spend the rest of my life in the British Museum and be happy. . . .

JAMES (*getting up*). All right, we'll try you in the office. I expect you want a holiday first, though.

PHILIP (*getting up*). My dear uncle, this is holiday. Being in London is holiday. Buying an evening paper—wearing a waistcoat again—running after a bus—anything—it's all holiday.

JAMES. All right, then, come along with me now, and I'll introduce you to Mr. Bamford.

PHILIP. Right. Who's he?

JAMES. Our manager. A little stiff, but a very good fellow. He'll be delighted to hear that you are coming into the firm.

PHILIP (*smiling*). Perhaps I'd better bring my revolver, in case he isn't.

JAMES (*laughing with forced heartiness as they go together to the door*). Ha, ha! A good joke that! Ha, ha, ha! A good joke—but only a joke, of course. Ha, ha! He, he, he!

[PHILIP *goes out.* JAMES, *following him, turns at the door, and looks round the room in a bewildered way. Was it a dream, or wasn't it? He will never be quite certain.*

BELINDA

AN APRIL FOLLY IN THREE ACTS

CHARACTERS.

BELINDA TREMAYNE.
DELIA (*her daughter*).
HAROLD BAXTER.
CLAUDE DEVENISH.
JOHN TREMAYNE.
BETTY.

The action takes place in Belinda's country-house
in Devonshire at the end of April.

THIS play was first produced by Mr. Dion Boucicault at
the New Theatre on April 8, 1918, with the following
cast :

Belinda Tremayne	-	IRENE VANBRUGH.
Delia - -	-	ISOBEL ELSOM.
Harold Baxter -	-	DION BOUCICAULT.
Claude Devenish	-	DENNIS NEILSON-TERRY.
John Tremayne -	-	BEN WEBSTER.
Betty - -	-	ANNE WALDEN.

BELINDA

ACT I

It is a lovely April afternoon—a foretaste of summer—in BELINDA'S *garden.*

BETTY, *a middle-aged servant, is fastening a hammock—its first appearance this year—between two trees at the back. In front of these there is a solid oak garden-table, with a comfortable chair on the right of it and a straight-backed one on the left. There are books, papers, and magazines on the table.* BELINDA, *of whom we shall know more presently, is on the other side of the open French-windows which lead into the garden, talking to* BETTY.

BELINDA (*from inside the house*). Are you sure you're tying it up tightly enough, Betty?

BETTY. Yes, ma'am; I think it's firm.

BELINDA. Because I'm not the fairy I used to be.

BETTY (*trying the knots at the other end of the hammock*). Yes, ma'am; it's quite firm this end too.

BELINDA. It's not the ends I'm frightened of; it's the middle where the weight's coming. (*She comes into the garden.*) It looks very nice.

BETTY. Yes, ma'am.

BELINDA (*trying the middle of it with her hand*). I asked them at the Stores if they were quite *sure* it would bear me, and they said it would take anything up to—I forget how many tons. I know I thought it was rather rude of them. (*Looking at it anxiously*) How does one get in? So trying to be a sailor!

BETTY. I think you sit in it, ma'am, and then (*explaining with her hands*) throw your legs over.

BELINDA. I see. (*She sits gingerly in the hammock, and then, with a sudden flutter of white, does what* BETTY *suggests.*) Yes. (*Regretfully*) I'm afraid that was rather wasted on you, Betty. We must have some spectators next time.

BETTY. Yes, ma'am.

BELINDA. Cushions. (*She arranges them at her back with* BETTY's *help. With a sigh of comfort*) There! Now then, Betty, about callers.

BETTY. Yes, ma'am.

BELINDA. If Mr. Baxter calls—he is the rather prim gentleman——

BETTY. Yes, ma'am; the one who's been here several times before.

BELINDA. Yes. Well, if he calls, you'll say, "Not at home."

BETTY. Yes, ma'am.

BELINDA. He will say, "Oh—er—oh—er—really." Then you'll smile very sweetly and say, "I beg your pardon, was it Mr. *Baxter?*" And he'll say, "Yes!" and you'll say, "Oh, I beg your pardon, sir; *this* way, please."

BETTY. Yes, ma'am.

BELINDA. That's right, Betty. Well now, if Mr. Devenish calls—he is the rather poetical gentleman——

BETTY. Yes, ma'am; the one who's always coming here.

BELINDA. Yes. Well, if he calls you'll say, "Not at home."

BETTY. Yes, ma'am.

BELINDA. He'll immediately throw down his bunch of flowers and dive despairingly into the moat. You'll stop him, just as he is going in, and say, " I beg your pardon, sir, was it Mr. *Devenish ?"* And he will say, " Yes !" and you will say, " Oh, I beg your pardon, sir ; *this* way, please."

BETTY. Yes, ma'am. And suppose they both call together ?

BELINDA. We won't suppose anything so exciting, Betty.

BETTY. No, ma'am. And suppose any other gentleman calls ?

BELINDA (*with a sigh*). There aren't any other gentlemen.

BETTY. It might be a clergyman, come to ask for a subscription like.

BELINDA. If it's a clergyman, Betty, I shall—I shall want your assistance out of the hammock first.

BETTY. Yes, ma'am.

BELINDA. That's all. To anybody else I'm not at home. Oh, just give me that little green book. (*Pointing to books on the table*) The one at the bottom there—that's the one. (BETTY *gives it to her.*) Thank you. (*Reading the title*) " The Lute of Love," by Claude Devenish. (*To herself as she turns the pages*) It doesn't seem much for half a crown when you think of the *Daily Telegraph.* . . . Lute . . . Lute. . . . I should have quite a pretty mouth if I kept on saying that. (*With a great deal of expression*) Lute ! (*She pats her mouth back.*)

BETTY. Is that all, ma'am ?

BELINDA. That's all. (BETTY *prepares to go.*) Oh, what am I thinking of ! (*Waving to the table*) I want that review; I think it's the blue one. (*As* BETTY *begins to look*) It has an article by Mr. Baxter on the " Rise of Lunacy in the Eastern Counties "—yes, that's the one. I'd better have that too; I'm just at the most exciting place. You shall have it after *me*, Betty.

BETTY. Is that all, ma'am?

BELINDA. Yes, that really is all.

[BETTY *goes into the house.*

BELINDA (*reading to herself*). " It is a matter of grave concern to all serious students of social problems——" (*Putting the review down and shaking her head gently*) But not in April. (*Lazily opening the book and reading*) " Tell me where is love "—well, that's the question, isn't it? (*She puts the book down, gives a sigh of happiness, and lazily closes her eyes.* DELIA *comes into the garden, from Paris. She is decidedly a modern girl, pretty and self-possessed. Her hair is half-way up; waiting for her birthday, perhaps. She sees her mother suddenly, stops, and then goes on tiptoe to the head of the hammock. She smiles and kisses her mother on the forehead.* BELINDA, *looking supremely unconscious, goes on sleeping.* DELIA *kisses her lightly again.* BELINDA *wakes up with an extraordinarily natural start, and is just about to say,* " Oh, Mr. Devenish—you mustn't !"—when she *sees* DELIA.) Delia!

DELIA. Well, mummy, aren't you glad to see me?

BELINDA. My darling child!

(*They kiss each other frantically.*)

DELIA. Say you're glad.

BELINDA (*sitting up*). My darling, I'm absolutely—— Hold the hammock while I get out, dear; we don't want an accident. (*Getting out with* DELIA'S *help*) They're all right when you're there, and they'll bear two tons, but they're horrid getting in and out of. (*Kissing her again*) Darling, it really *is* you?

DELIA. Oh, it is jolly seeing you again.   I believe you were asleep.

BELINDA (*with dignity*). Certainly not, child. (*Picking up the review*) I was reading "The Nineteenth Century"— (*with an air*) and after. (*Earnestly*) Darling, wasn't it next Thursday you were coming back ?

DELIA. No, this Thursday, silly.

BELINDA (*penitently*). Oh, my darling, and I was going over to Paris to bring you home.

DELIA. I half expected you.

BELINDA. So confusing their both being called Thursday.   And you were leaving school for the very last time.   If you don't forgive me, Delia, I shall cry.

DELIA (*stroking her hand fondly*). Silly mother !

(BELINDA *sits down in a basket chair and* DELIA *sits on a table next to her.*)

BELINDA. Isn't it a lovely day for April, darling ?   I've wanted to say that to somebody all day, and you're the first person who's given me the chance.   Oh, I said it to Betty, but she only said, "Yes, ma'am."

DELIA. Poor mother !

BELINDA (*jumping up suddenly and kissing* DELIA *again*). I simply must have another one.   And to think that you're never going back to school any more. (*Looking at her fondly*) Darling, you *are* looking pretty.

DELIA. Am I ?

BELINDA. Lovely. (*Going back to her seat*) And now you're going to stay with me for just as long as you want a mother. (*Anxiously*) Darling, you didn't mind being sent away to school, did you ?   It *is* the usual thing, you know.

DELIA. Silly mother ! of course it is.

BELINDA (*relieved*). I'm so glad you think so too.

DELIA. Have you been very lonely without me ?

BELINDA. Very.

DELIA (*holding up a finger*). The truth, mummy!

BELINDA. I've missed you horribly, Delia. (*Primly*) The absence of female companionship of the requisite——

DELIA. Are you really all alone?

BELINDA (*smiling mysteriously*). Well, not always, of course.

DELIA (*excitedly, as she slips off the table*). Mummy, I believe you're being bad again.

BELINDA. Really, darling, you forget that I'm old enough to be—in fact, am—your mother.

DELIA (*nodding her head*). You *are* being bad.

BELINDA (*rising with dignity and drawing herself up to her full height*). My child, that is not the way to—— Oh I say, what a lot taller I am than you!

DELIA. And prettier.

BELINDA (*fluttering her eyelids*). Oh, do you think so? (*Firmly*) Don't be silly, child.

DELIA (*holding up a finger*). Now tell me all that's been happening here at once.

BELINDA (*with a sigh*). And I was just going to ask you how you were getting on with your French.

DELIA. Bother French! You've been having a much more interesting time than I have, so you've got to tell.

BELINDA (*with a happy sigh*). O-oh! (*She sinks back into her chair.*)

DELIA. Is it like the Count at Scarborough?

BELINDA (*surprised and pained*). My darling, what *do* you mean?

DELIA. Don't you remember the Count who kept proposing to you at Scarborough? I do.

BELINDA (*reproachfully*). Dear one, you were the

merest child, paddling about on the beach and digging castles.

DELIA (*smiling to herself*). I was old enough to notice the Count.

BELINDA (*sadly*). And I'd bought her a perfectly new spade ! How one deceives oneself !

DELIA. And then there was the M.P. who proposed at Windermere.

BELINDA. Yes, dear, but it wasn't seconded—I mean he never got very far with it.

DELIA. And the artist in Wales.

BELINDA. Darling child, what a memory you have No wonder your teachers are pleased with you.

DELIA (*settling herself comfortably*). Now tell me all about this one.

BELINDA (*meekly*). Which one ?

DELIA (*excitedly*). Oh, are there lots ?

BELINDA (*severely*). Only two.

DELIA. Two ! You abandoned woman !

BELINDA. It's something in the air, darling. I've never been in Devonshire in April before.

DELIA. Is it really serious this time ?

BELINDA (*pained*). I wish you wouldn't say *this* time, Delia. It sounds so unromantic. If you'd only put it into French—*cette fois*—it sounds so much better. *Cette fois.* (*Parentally*) When one's daughter has just returned from an expensive schooling in Paris, one likes to feel——

DELIA. What I meant, dear, was, am I to have a stepfather at last ?

BELINDA. Now you're being *too* French, darling.

DELIA. Why, do you still think father may be alive ?

BELINDA. Why not ? It's only eighteen years since he left us, and he was quite a young man then.

DELIA. Yes, but surely you'd have heard from him in all those years, if he'd been alive?

BELINDA. Well, he hasn't heard from *me*, and I'm still alive.

DELIA (*looking earnestly at her mother*). I shall never understand it.

BELINDA. Understand what?

DELIA. Were you as heavenly when you were young as you are now?

BELINDA (*rapturously*). Oh, I was sweet!

DELIA. And yet he left you after only six months.

BELINDA (*rather crossly*). I wish you wouldn't keep on saying he left me. I left him too.

DELIA. Why?

BELINDA (*smiling to herself*). Well, you see, he was quite certain he knew how to manage women, and I was quite certain I knew how to manage men. (*Thoughtfully*) If only one of us had been certain, it would have been all right.

DELIA (*seriously*). What really happened, mummy? I'm grown up now, so I think you ought to tell me.

BELINDA (*thoughtfully*). That was about all, you know . . . except for his beard.

DELIA. Had he a beard? How funny!

BELINDA. Yes, dear, it was; but he never would see it. He took it quite seriously.

DELIA. And did you say dramatically, " If you really loved me, you'd take it off"?

BELINDA (*apologetically*). I'm afraid I did, darling.

DELIA. And what did *he* say?

BELINDA. He said—*very* rudely—that, if I loved *him*, I'd do my hair in a different way.

DELIA. How ridiculous!

BELINDA (*touching her hair*). Of course, I didn't do it

like this then. (*With a sigh*) I suppose we never ought to have married, really.

DELIA. Why did you?

BELINDA. Mother rather wanted it. (*Solemnly*) Delia, never get married because your mother—— Oh, I forgot; *I'm* your mother.

DELIA. And I don't want a better one. . . . And so you left each other?

BELINDA. Yes.

DELIA. Didn't you tell him there was going to be a Me?

BELINDA. Oh no!

DELIA. I wonder why not?

BELINDA. Well, you see, if I had, he might have wanted to stay.

DELIA. But——

BELINDA (*hurt*). If he didn't want to stay for *me*, I didn't want him to stay for *you*. (*Penitently*) Forgive me, darling, but I didn't know you very well then. (DELIA *jumps off the table and hugs her mother impetuously.*) We've been very happy together, haven't we?

DELIA (*going back to her seat*). I should think we have.

BELINDA. I don't want to deny you anything, and, of course, if you'd like a stepfather (*looking down modestly*) or two——

DELIA. Oh, you *have* been enjoying yourself.

BELINDA. Only you see how awkward it would be if Jack turned up in the middle of the wedding, like— like Eugene Aram.

DELIA. Enoch Arden, darling.

BELINDA. It's very confusing their having the same initials. Perhaps I'd better call them both E. A. in future and then I shall be safe. Well, anyhow it would be awkward, darling, wouldn't it? Not that I should know him from Adam after all these years—except for a mole on his left arm.

DELIA. Perhaps Adam had a mole.

BELINDA. No, darling; you're thinking of Noah. He had two.

DELIA (*thoughtfully*). I wonder what would happen if you met somebody whom you really did fall in love with.

BELINDA (*reproachfully*). Now you're being serious, and it's April.

DELIA. Aren't these two—the present two—serious?

BELINDA. Oh no! They think they are, but they aren't a bit, really. Besides, I'm doing them such a lot of good. I'm sure they'd hate to marry me, but they love to think they're in love with me, and—*I* love it, and—and *they* love it, and—and we *all* love it.

DELIA. You really are the biggest, darlingest baby who ever lived. Do say I shan't spoil your lovely times.

BELINDA (*surprised*). Spoil them? Why, you'll make them more lovely than ever.

DELIA. Well, but do they know you have a grown-up daughter?

BELINDA (*suddenly realizing*). Oh!

DELIA. It doesn't really matter, because you don't look a day more than thirty.

BELINDA (*absently*). No. (*Hurriedly*) I mean, how sweet of you—only——

DELIA. What?

BELINDA (*playing with her rings*). Well, one of them, Mr. Baxter—Harold—(*she looks quickly up at* DELIA *and down again in pretty affectation, but she is really laughing at herself all the time*) he writes statistical articles for the

Reviews—percentages and all those things. He's just
the sort of man, if he knew that I was your mother, to
work it out that I was *more* than thirty. The other one,
Mr. Devenish—Claude—(*she looks up and down as
before*) he's rather, rather poetical. He thinks I came
straight from heaven—last week.

DELIA (*jumping up*). I think *I'd* better go straight
back to Paris.

BELINDA (*jumping up and holding her firmly by the arms*).
You will do nothing of the sort. You will take off that
hat—(*she lets go of one arm and begins to take out the pin*)
which is a perfect duck, and I don't know why I didn't
say so before—(*she puts the hat down on the table*) and
'et me take a good look at you (*she does so*), and kiss
you (*she does so*), and then we'll go to your room and
unpack and have a lovely talk about clothes. And then
we'll have tea.

BETTY *comes in.*

BELINDA. And now here's Betty coming in to upset
all our delightful plans, just when we've made them.

DELIA. How are you, Betty? I've left school.

BETTY. Very nicely, thank you, miss. You've grown.

BELINDA (*patting the top of* DELIA's *head*). I'm much
taller than she is. . . . Well, Betty what is it?

BETTY. The two gentlemen, Mr. Baxter and Mr.
Devenish, have both called together, ma'am.

BELINDA (*excited*). Oh! How—how very simultaneous
of them!

DELIA (*eagerly*). Oh, do let me see them!

BELINDA. Darling, you'll see plenty of them before
you've finished. (*To* BETTY) What have you done with
them?

BETTY. They're waiting in the hall, ma'am, while I
said I would see if you were at home.

BELINDA. All right, Betty. Give me two minutes and
then show them out here.

BETTY. Yes, ma'am.   [*Exit.*

BELINDA. They can't do much harm to each other in
two minutes.

DELIA (*taking her hat*). Well, I'll go and unpack. You
really won't mind my coming down afterwards?

BELINDA. Of course not. (*A little awkwardly*) Darling
one, I wonder if you'd mind—just at first—being introduced as my niece. You see, I expect they're in a bad
temper already, having come here together, and we
don't want to spoil their day entirely.

DELIA (*smiling*). I'll be your mother if you like.

BELINDA. Oh no, that wouldn't do, because then
Mr. Baxter would feel that he ought to ask your
permission before paying his attentions to me. He's
just that sort of man. A niece is so safe—however
good you are at statistics, you can't really prove anything.

DELIA. All right, mummy.

BELINDA (*enjoying herself*). You'd like to be called by
a different name, wouldn't you? There's something so
thrilling about taking a false name. Such a lot of
adventures begin like that. How would you like to be
Miss Robinson, darling? It's a nice easy one to
remember. (*Persuasively*) And you shall put your hair
up so as to feel more disguised. What fun we're going
to have!

DELIA. You baby! All right, then, I'm Miss Robinson, your favourite niece. (*She moves towards the house.*)

BELINDA. How sweet of you! Oh, I'm coming with
you to do your hair. You don't think you're going to
be allowed to do it yourself, when so much depends
on it, and husbands leave you because of it, and——

                              [*They go in together.*

BETTY *comes from the other side of the house into the garden, followed by* MR. BAXTER *and* MR. DEVENISH. MR. BAXTER *is forty-five, prim and erect, with close-rimmed moustache and side-whiskers. His clothes are dark and he wears a bowler-hat.* MR. DEVENISH *is a long-haired good-looking boy in a négligé costume; perhaps twenty-two years old, and very scornful of the world.*

BETTY (*looking about her surprised*). The mistress was here a moment ago. I expect she'll be back directly, if you'll just wait. [*She goes back into the house.*

(MR. BAXTER *puts his bowler-hat firmly on his head and sits down very stiffly and upright in a chair on the left-hand side of the table.* DEVENISH *throws his felt hat on to the table and walks about inquisitively. He sees the review in the hammock and picks it up.*)

DEVENISH. Good heavens, Baxter, she's been reading your article !

BAXTER. I daresay she's not the only one.

DEVENISH. That's only guesswork ; you don't know of anyone else.

BAXTER. How many people, may I ask, have bought your poems ?

DEVENISH (*loftily*). I don't write for the mob.

BAXTER. I think I may say that of my own work.

DEVENISH. Baxter, I don't want to disappoint you, but I have reluctantly come to the conclusion that you *are* one of the mob. (*Annoyed*) Dash it ! what are you doing in the country at all in a bowler-hat ?

BAXTER. If I wanted to be personal, I could say, " Why don't you get your hair cut ?" Only that form of schoolboy humour doesn't appeal to me.

DEVENISH. This is not a personal matter ; I am

protesting on behalf of nature. What do the birds and the flowers and the beautiful trees think of your hat?

BAXTER. If one began to ask oneself what the birds thought of things—— (*He pauses.*)

DEVENISH. Well, and why shouldn't one ask oneself? It is better than asking oneself what the Stock Exchange thinks of things.

BAXTER. Well (*looking up at* DEVENISH'S *extravagant hair*), it's the nesting season. (*Suddenly*) Ha! ha! ha! ha! ha! ha!

DEVENISH (*hastily smoothing it down*). Really, Baxter, you're vulgar. (*He turns away and resumes his promenading. Suddenly he sees his book on the grass beneath the hammock and makes a dash for it.*) Ha, my book! (*Gloating over it*) Baxter, she reads my book.

BAXTER. I suppose you gave her a copy.

DEVENISH (*exultingly*). Yes, I gave her a copy. My next book will be hers and hers alone.

BAXTER. Then let me say that, in my opinion, you took a very great liberty.

DEVENISH. Liberty! And this from a man who is continually forcing his unwelcome statistics upon her.

BAXTER. At any rate, I flatter myself that there is no suggestion of impropriety in anything that *I* write.

DEVENISH. I'm not so sure about that, Baxter.

BAXTER. What do you mean, sir?

DEVENISH. Did you read *The Times* this month on the new reviews?

BAXTER. Well?

DEVENISH. Oh, nothing. It just said, " Mr. Baxter's statistics are extremely suggestive." I haven't read them, so of course I don't know what you've been up to.

BAXTER (*turning away in disgust*). Pah!

DEVENISH. Poor old Baxter! (*He wanders about the garden again, and, having picked a flower, comes to rest against one of the trees from which the hammock is swung. He leans against this and regards the flower thoughtfully.*) Baxter——

BAXTER (*crossly*). I wish you wouldn't keep calling me " Baxter."

DEVENISH. Harold.

BAXTER. It is only by accident—an accident which we both deplore—that we have met at all, and in any case I am a considerably older man than yourself.

DEVENISH. Mr. Baxter—father—I have a proposal to make. We will leave it to this beautiful flower to decide which of us the lady loves.

BAXTER (*turning round*). Eh?

DEVENISH (*pulling off the petals*). She loves me, she loves Mr. Baxter, she loves me, she loves Mr. Baxter—Heaven help her!—she loves me——

BELINDA (*at the garden door*). What *are* you doing, Mr. Devenish?

DEVENISH (*throwing away the flower and bowing very low*). My lady.

BAXTER (*removing his bowler-hat stiffly*). Good-afternoon, Mrs. Tremayne.

(*She gives her left hand to* DEVENISH, *who kisses it, and her right to* BAXTER, *who shakes it.*)

BELINDA. How nice of you both to come!

BAXTER. Mr. Devenish and I are inseparable— apparently.

BELINDA. You haven't told me what you were doing, Mr. Devenish. Was it " This year, next year "? or " Silk, satin——"

DEVENISH. My lady, it was even more romantic than that. I have the honour to announce to your ladyship that Mr. Baxter is to be a sailor.

BELINDA (*to* BAXTER). Doesn't he talk nonsense?

BAXTER. He'll grow out of it. I did.

BELINDA. Oh, I hope not. I love talking nonsense, and I'm ever so old. (*As they both start forward to protest*) Now which one of you will say it first?

DEVENISH. You are as old as the stars and as young as the dawn.

BAXTER. You are ten years younger than I am.

BELINDA. What sweet things to say! I don't know which I like best.

DEVENISH. Where will my lady sit?

BELINDA. I will recline in the hammock, an it please thee, my lord—only it's rather awkward getting in, Mr. Baxter. Perhaps you'd both better look at the tulips for a moment.

BAXTER. Oh—ah—yes. (*He puts his hat on and turns his back to the hammock.*)

DEVENISH. If only——

BELINDA. You'd better not say anything, Mr. Devenish. Keep it for your next volume. (*He turns away.*) One, two, three—that was better than last time. (*They turn round to see her safely in the hammock.* DEVENISH *leans against the tree at her feet, and* BAXTER *draws back the chair from the right side of the table and turns it round towards her. He presses his hat more firmly on and sits down.*) I wonder if either of you can guess what I've been reading this afternoon.

DEVENISH (*looking at her lovingly*). I know.

BELINDA (*giving him a fleeting look*). How did you know? (*To* BAXTER) Yes, Mr. Baxter, it was your article I was reading. If you'd come five minutes earlier you'd have found me wrestling—I mean revelling in it.

BAXTER. I am very greatly honoured, Mrs. Tremayne.

Ah—it seemed to me a very interesting curve showing the rise and fall of——

BELINDA. I hadn't got up to the curves. They *are* interesting, aren't they? They are really more in Mr. Devenish's line. (*To* DEVENISH) Mr. Devenish, it was a great disappointment to me that all the poems in your book seemed to be written to somebody else.

DEVENISH. It was before I met you, lady. They were addressed to the goddess of my imagination. It is only in these last few weeks that I have discovered her.

BELINDA. And discovered she was dark and not fair.

DEVENISH. She will be dark in my next volume.

BELINDA. Oh, how nice of her!

BAXTER (*kindly*). You should write a real poem to Mrs. Tremayne.

BELINDA (*excitedly*). Oh do! "To Belinda." I don't know what rhymes, except cinder. You could say your heart was like a cinder—all burnt up.

DEVENISH (*pained*). I'm afraid that is a cockney rhyme.

BELINDA. How thrilling! I've never been to Hampstead Heath.

DEVENISH. "Belinda." It is too beautiful to rhyme with anything but itself.

BELINDA. Fancy! But what about Tremayne? (*Singing*) Oh, I am Mrs. Tremayne, and I don't want to marry again.

DEVENISH (*protesting*). My lady!

BAXTER (*protesting*). Belinda!

BELINDA (*pointing excitedly to* BAXTER). There, that's the first time he's called me Belinda!

DEVENISH. Are you serious?

BELINDA. Not as a rule,

DEVENISH. You're not going to marry again?

BELINDA. Well, who could I marry?

DEVENISH
and   }(*together*). Me!
BAXTER

BELINDA (*dropping her eyes modestly*). But this is England.

BAXTER. Mrs. Tremayne, I claim the right of age—of my greater years—to speak first.

BELINDA (*kindly to* DEVENISH). You can speak afterwards, Mr. Devenish. It's so awkward when you both speak together.

BAXTER. Mrs. Tremayne, I am a man of substantial position, and perhaps I may say of some repute in serious circles. All that I have, whether of material or mental endowment, I lay at your feet, together with an admiration which I cannot readily put into words. As my wife I think you would be happy, and I feel that with you by my side I could achieve even greater things.

BELINDA. How sweet of you! But I ought to tell you that I'm no good at figures.

DEVENISH (*protesting*). My lady——

BELINDA. I don't mean what you mean, Mr. Devenish. You wait till it's your turn. (*To* BAXTER) Yes?

BAXTER. I ask you to marry me, Belinda.

BELINDA (*settling herself happily and closing her eyes*). O-oh! . . . Now it's *your* turn, Mr. Devenish.

DEVENISH (*excitedly*). Money—thank Heaven, I have no money. Reputation—thank Heaven, I have no reputation. What can I offer you? Dreams—nothing but dreams. Come with me and I will show you the world through my dreams. What can I give you? Youth, freedom, beauty——

BAXTER. Debts.

BELINDA (*still with her eyes shut*). You mustn't interrupt, Mr. Baxter.

DEVENISH. Belinda, marry me and I will open your eyes to the beauty of the world. Come to me!

BELINDA (*happily*). O-oh! You've got such different ways of putting things. How can I choose between you?

DEVENISH. Then you will marry one of us?

BELINDA. You know I really *oughtn't* to.

BAXTER. I don't see why not.

BELINDA. Well, there's just a little difficulty in the way.

DEVENISH. What is it? I will remove it. For you I could remove anything—yes, even Baxter. (*He looks at* BAXTER, *who is sitting more solidly than ever in his chair.*)

BELINDA. And anyhow I should have to choose between you.

DEVENISH (*in a whisper*). Choose me.

BAXTER (*stiffly*). Mrs. Tremayne does not require any prompting. A fair field and let the best man win.

DEVENISH (*going across and slapping the astonished* BAXTER *on the back*). Ay, let the best man win! Well spoken, Baxter. (*To* BELINDA) Send us out into the world upon some knightly quest, lady, and let the victor be rewarded.

BAXTER. I—er—ought to say that I should be unable to go very far. I have an engagement to speak at Newcastle on the 21st.

DEVENISH. Baxter, I will take no unfair advantage of you. Let the beard of the Lord Mayor of Newcastle be the talisman that my lady demands; I am satisfied.

BAXTER. This sort of thing is entirely contrary to my usual mode of life, but I will not be outfaced by a mere boy. (*Slamming his bowler-hat on the table*) I am prepared.

DEVENISH. Speak, lady.

BELINDA (*speaking in a deep mysterious voice*). Gentlemen, ye put wild thoughts into my head. In sooth, I am minded to send ye forth upon a quest that is passing strange. Know ye that there is a maid journeyed hither, hight Robinson—whose—(*in her natural voice*) what's the old for aunt?

BAXTER (*hopefully*). Mother's sister.

BELINDA. You know, I think I shall have to explain this in ordinary language. You won't mind very much, will you, Mr. Devenish?

DEVENISH. It is the spirit of this which matters, not the language which clothes it.

BELINDA. Oh, I'm so glad you think so. Well, now about Miss Robinson. She's my niece and she's just come to stay with me, and—poor girl—she's lost her father. Absolutely lost him. He disappeared ever such a long time ago, and poor Miss Robinson—Delia—naturally wants to find him. Poor girl! she can't think where he is.

DEVENISH (*nobly*). I will find him.

BELINDA. Oh, thank you, Mr. Devenish; Miss Robinson would be so much obliged.

BAXTER. What have we to go upon? Beyond the fact that his name is Robinson——

BELINDA. I shouldn't go on that too much. You see, he may easily have changed it by now. He was never very much of a Robinson. Nothing to do with Peter or any of those.

DEVENISH. I will find him.

BAXTER. Well, can you tell us what he's like?

BELINDA. Well, it's such a long time since I saw him. (*Looking down modestly*) Of course, I was quite a girl then. The only thing I know for certain is that he has a mole on his left arm about here. (*She indicates a spot just below the elbow.*)

DEVENISH (*folding his arms and looking nobly upwards*). I will find him.

BAXTER. I am bound to inform you, Mrs. Tremayne, that even a trained detective could not give you very much hope in such a case. However, I will keep a look-out for him, and, of course, if——

DEVENISH. Fear not, lady, I will find him.

BAXTER (*annoyed*). Yes, you keep on saying that, but what have you got to go on?

DEVENISH (*grandly*). Faith! The faith which moves mountains.

BELINDA. Yes, and this is only just one small mole-hill, Mr. Baxter.

BAXTER. Yes, but still——

BELINDA. S'sh! here is Miss Robinson. If Mr. Devenish will hold the hammock while I alight—we don't want an accident—I can introduce you. (*He helps her to get out.*) Thank you. Delia darling, this is Mr. Baxter—and Mr. Devenish. My niece, Miss Robinson——

DELIA. How do you do?

BELINDA. Miss Robinson has just come over from France. *Mon Dieu, quel pays!*

BAXTER. I hope you had a good crossing, Miss Robinson.

DELIA. Oh, I never mind about the crossing. Aunt Belinda—— (*She stops and smiles.*)

BELINDA. Yes, dear?

DELIA. I believe tea is almost ready. I want mine, and I'm sure Mr. Baxter's hungry. Mr. Devenish scorns food, I expect.

DEVENISH (*hurt*). Why do you say that?

DELIA. Aren't you a poet?

BELINDA. Yes, darling, but that doesn't prevent him eating. He'll be absolutely lyrical over Betty's sandwiches.

DEVENISH. You won't deny me that inspiration, I hope, Miss Robinson.

BELINDA. Well, let's go and see what they're like. (DELIA *and* DEVENISH *begin to move towards the house.*) Mr. Baxter, just a moment.

BAXTER. Yes?

BELINDA (*secretly*). Not a word to her about Mr. Robinson. It must be a surprise for her.

BAXTER. Quite so, I understand.

BELINDA. That's right. (*Raising her voice*) Oh, Mr. Devenish.

DEVENISH. Yes, Mrs. Tremayne? (*He comes back.*)

BELINDA (*secretly*). Not a word to her about Mr. Robinson. It must be a surprise for her.

DEVENISH. Of course! I shouldn't dream—— (*Indignantly*) Robinson! *What* an unsuitable name!

[BAXTER *and* DELIA *are just going into the house.*

BELINDA (*dismissing* DEVENISH). All right, I'll catch you up.

[DEVENISH *goes after the other two.*

(*Left alone,* BELINDA *laughs happily to herself, and then begins to look rather aimlessly about her. She comes to the hammock, picks out her handkerchief, says,* "Ah, there you are!" *and puts it away. She goes slowly back to the house, turns her head just as she comes to the door, and comes slowly back again. She stops at the table looking down the garden.*)

BELINDA (*to herself*). Have you lost yourself, or something? No; the latch is this side. . . . Yes, that's right.

TREMAYNE *comes in.   He has been knocking about the world
    for eighteen years, and is very much a man, though he
    has kept his manners.   His hair is greying a little a.
    the sides, and he looks the forty-odd that he is.   With-
    out his moustache and beard he is very different from
    the boy* BELINDA *married.* .

TREMAYNE (*with his hat in his hand*). I'm afraid I'm
trespassing.

BELINDA (*winningly*). But it's such a pretty garden,
isn't it?

TREMAYNE (*rather confused*). I—I beg your pardon,
I—er——

> (*He is wondering if it can possibly be she.* BELINDA
> *thinks his confusion is due to the fact that he is
> trespassing, and hastens to put him at his ease.*)

BELINDA. I should have done the same myself, you
know.

TREMAYNE (*pulling himself together*). Oh, but you
mustn't think I just came in because I liked the
garden——

BELINDA (*clapping her hands*). No; but say you do like
it, quick.

TREMAYNE. It's lovely and——   (*He hesitates.*)

BELINDA (*hopefully*). Yes?

TREMAYNE (*with conviction*). Yes, it's lovely.

BELINDA (*with that happy sigh of hers*). O-oh! . .
Now tell me what really did happen?

TREMAYNE. I was on my way to Marytown——

BELINDA. To where?

TREMAYNE. Marytown.

BELINDA. Oh, you mean Mariton.

TREMAYNE. Do I?

BELINDA. Yes; we always call it Mariton down here.
(*Earnestly*) You don't mind, do you?

TREMAYNE (*smiling*). Not a bit.

BELINDA. Just say it—to see if you've got it right.

TREMAYNE. Mariton.

BELINDA (*shaking her head*). Oh no, that's quite wrong. Try it again. (*With a rustic accent*) Mariton.

TREMAYNE. Mariton.

BELINDA. Yes, that's much better. . . . (*As if it were he who had interrupted*) Well, do go on.

TREMAYNE. I'm afraid it isn't much of an apology really. I saw what looked like a private road, but what I rather hoped wasn't, and—well, I thought I'd risk it. I do hope you'll forgive me.

BELINDA. Oh, but I love people seeing my garden. Are you staying in Mariton?

TREMAYNE. I think so. Oh yes, decidedly.

BELINDA. Well, perhaps the next time the road won't feel so private.

TREMAYNE. How charming of you! (*He feels he must know.*) Are you Mrs. Tremayne by any chance?

BELINDA. Yes.

TREMAYNE (*nodding to himself*). Yes.

BELINDA. How did you know?

TREMAYNE (*hastily inventing*). They use you as a signpost in the village. Past Mrs. Tremayne's house and then bear to the left——

BELINDA. And you couldn't go past it?

TREMAYNE. I'm afraid I couldn't. Thank you so much for not minding. Well, I must be getting on, I have trespassed quite enough.

BELINDA (*regretfully*). And you haven't really seen the garden yet.

TREMAYNE. If you won't mind my going on this way, I shall see some more on my way out.

BELINDA. Please do. It likes being looked at. (*With the faintest suggestion of demureness*) All pretty things do.

TREMAYNE. Thank you very much. Er—— (*He hesitates.*)

BELINDA (*helpfully*). Yes ?

TREMAYNE. I wonder if you'd mind very much if I called one day to thank you formally for the lesson you gave me in pronunciation ?

BELINDA (*gravely*). Yes, I almost think you ought to. I think it's the correct thing to do.

TREMAYNE (*contentedly*). Thank you very much, Mrs. Tremayne.

BELINDA. You'll come in quite formally by the front-door next time, won't you, because—because that seems the only chance of my getting to know your name.

TREMAYNE. Oh, I beg your pardon. My name is—er —er—Robinson.

BELINDA (*laughing*). How very odd !

TREMAYNE (*startled*). Odd ?

BELINDA. Yes ; we have someone called Robinson staying in the house. I wonder if she's any relation ?

TREMAYNE (*hastily*). Oh no, no. No, she couldn't be. I have no relations called Robinson—not to speak of.

BELINDA (*holding out her hand*). You must tell me all about your relations when you come and call, Mr. Robinson.

TREMAYNE. I think we can find something better worth talking about than that.

BELINDA. Do you think so ? (*He says " Yes " with his eyes, bows, and goes off down the garden.* BELINDA *stays looking after him, and then gives that happy sigh of hers, only even more so*) O-oh !

Enter BETTY.

BETTY. If you please, ma'am, Miss Delia says, are you coming in to tea ?

BELINDA (*looking straight in front of her, and taking no*

notice of BETTY, *in a happy, dreamy voice*) Betty, . . .
about callers. . . . If Mr. Robinson calls—he's the
handsome gentleman who hasn't been here before—you
will say, "Not at home." And he will say, "Oh!" And
you will say, "I beg your pardon, sir, was it Mr.
Robinson?" And he will say, "Yes!" And you will say,
" Oh, I beg your pardon, sir——" (*Almost as if she were*
BETTY, *she begins to move towards the house*) "This way—"
(*she would be smiling an invitation over her shoulder to* MR.
ROBINSON, *if he were there, and she were* BETTY)—" please!"
(*And the abandoned woman goes in to tea.*)

ACT II

It is morning in BELINDA'S *hall, a low-roofed, oak-beamed place, comfortably furnished as a sitting-room. There is an inner and an outer front-door, both of which are open.*

DEVENISH, *who has just rung the bell, is waiting with a bouquet of violets between the two. Midway on the right is a door leading to a small room where hats and coats are kept. A door on the left leads toward the living-rooms.*

BETTY. Good-morning, sir.

DEVENISH. Good-morning. I am afraid this is an unceremonious hour for a call, but my sense of beauty urged me hither in defiance of convention.

BETTY. Yes, sir.

DEVENISH (*holding up his bouquet to* BETTY). See, the dew is yet lingering upon them; how could I let them wait until this afternoon?

BETTY. Yes, sir; but I think the mistress is out.

DEVENISH. They are not for your mistress; they are for Miss Delia.

BETTY. Oh, I beg your pardon, sir. If you will come in, I'll see if I can find her. (*She brings him in and goes away to find* DELIA.)

> (DEVENISH *tries a number of poses about the room for himself and his bouquet, and finally selects one against the right side of the door by which he has just come in.*)

157

Enter DELIA *from the door on the left.*

DELIA. Oh, good-morning, Mr. Devenish. I'm afraid my—er—aunt is out.

DEVENISH. I know, Miss Delia, I know.

DELIA. She'll be so sorry to have missed you. It is her day for you, isn't it?

DEVENISH. Her day for me?

DELIA. Yes; Mr. Baxter generally comes to-morrow, doesn't he?

DEVENISH. Miss Delia, if our friendship is to progress at all, it can only be on the distinct understanding that I take no interest whatever in Mr. Baxter's move-ments.

DELIA. Oh, I'm so sorry; I thought you knew. What lovely flowers! Are they for my aunt?

DEVENISH. To whom does one bring violets? To modest, shrinking, tender youth.

DELIA. I don't think we have anybody here like that.

DEVENISH (*with a bow*). Miss Delia, they are for you.

DELIA. Oh, how nice of you! But I'm afraid I oughtn't to take them from you under false pretences; I don't shrink.

DEVENISH. A fanciful way of putting it, perhaps. They are none the less for you.

DELIA. Well, it's awfully kind of you. I'm afraid I'm not a very romantic person. Aunt Belinda does all the romancing in our family.

DEVENISH. Your aunt is a very remarkable woman.

DELIA. She is. Don't you dare to say a word against her.

DEVENISH. My dear Miss Delia, nothing could be further from my thoughts. Why, am I not indebted to her for that great happiness which has come to me in these last few days?

DELIA (*surprised*). Good gracious ! and I didn't know anything about it.　But what about poor Mr. Baxter ?

DEVENISH (*stiffly*). I must beg that Mr. Baxter's name be kept out of our conversation.

DELIA. But I thought Mr. Baxter and you—do tell me what's happened.　I seem to have lost myself.

DEVENISH. What has happened, Miss Delia, is that I have learnt at last the secret that my heart has been striving to tell me for weeks past.　As soon as I saw that gracious lady, your aunt, I knew that I was in love.　Foolishly I took it for granted that it was she for whom my heart was thrilling.　How mistaken I was !　Directly you came, you opened my eyes, and now——

DELIA. Mr. Devenish, you don't say you're proposing to me ?

DEVENISH. I am.　I feel sure I am.　Delia, I love you.

DELIA. How exciting of you !

DEVENISH (*with a modest shrug*).　It's nothing ; I am a poet.

DELIA. You really want to marry me ?

DEVENISH. Such is my earnest wish.

DELIA. But what about my aunt ?

DEVENISH (*simply*). She will be my aunt-in-law.

DELIA. She'll be rather surprised.

DEVENISH. Delia, I will be frank with you.　I admit that I made Mrs. Tremayne an offer of marriage.

DELIA (*excitedly*). You really did ?　Was it that first afternoon I came?

DEVENISH. Yes.

DELIA. Oh, I wish I'd been there !

DEVENISH (*with dignity*). It is not my custom to propose in the presence of a third party.　It is true that on the occasion you mention a man called Baxter was on the lawn, but I regarded him no more than the old apple-tree or the flower-beds, or any other of the fixtures.

DELIA. What did she say?

DEVENISH. She accepted me conditionally.

DELIA. Oh, do tell me!

DEVENISH. It is rather an unhappy story. This man called Baxter in his vulgar way also made a proposal of marriage. Mrs. Tremayne was gracious enough to imply that she would marry whichever one of us fulfilled a certain condition.

DELIA. How sweet of her!

DEVENISH. It is my earnest hope, Miss Delia, that the man called Baxter will be the victor. As far as is consistent with honour, I shall endeavour to let Mr. Baxter win.

DELIA. What was the condition?

DEVENISH. That I am not at liberty to tell. It is, I understand, to be a surprise for you.

DELIA. How exciting! . . . Mr. Devenish, you have been very frank. May I be equally so? (DEVENISH *bows*.) Why do you wear your hair so long?

DEVENISH (*pleased*). You have noticed it?

DELIA. Well yes, I have.

DEVENISH. I wear it so to express my contempt for the conventions of so-called society.

DELIA. I always thought that people wore it very very short if they despised the conventions of society.

DEVENISH. I think that the mere fact that my hair annoys Mr. Baxter is sufficient justification for its length.

DELIA. But if it annoys me too?

DEVENISH (*heroically*). It shall go.

DELIA (*apologetically*). I told you I wasn't a very romantic person, didn't I? (*Kindly*) You can always grow it again if you fall in love with somebody else.

DEVENISH. That is cruel of you, Delia. I snall never fall in love again.

Enter BELINDA *in a hat.*

BELINDA. Why, it's Mr. Devenish! How nice of you to come so early in the morning! How is Mr. Baxter?

DEVENISH. I do not know, Mrs. Tremayne.

BELINDA (*to* DELIA). I got most of the things, Delia (*To* DEVENISH) "The things," Mr. Devenish, is my rather stuffy way of referring to all the delightful poems that you are going to eat to-night.

DEVENISH. I am looking forward to it immensely, Mrs. Tremayne.

BELINDA. I do hope I've got all your and Mr. Baxter's favourite dishes.

DEVENISH. I'm afraid Mr. Baxter and I are not likely to appreciate the same things.

BELINDA (*coyly*). Oh, Mr. Devenish! And you were so unanimous a few days ago.

DELIA. I think Mr. Devenish was referring entirely to things to eat.

BELINDA. I felt quite sad when I was buying the lamb cutlets. To think that, only a few days before, they had been frisking about with their mammas, and having poems written about them by Mr. Devenish. There! I'm giving away the whole dinner. Delia take him away before I tell him any more. We must keep some surprises for him.

DELIA (*to* DEVENISH *as she picks up the flowers*). Come along; we'll just put these in water first.

BELINDA (*wickedly*). Are those my flowers, Mr. Devenish?

DEVENISH (*after a little hesitation, with a bow which might refer to either of them*). They are for the most beautiful lady in the land.

BELINDA. Oh, how nice of you!

[DEVENISH *follows* DELIA *out through the door on the left.*

BELINDA (*unpinning her hat before a mirror*). I suppose he means Delia—bless them! (*She gives a few pats to her hair and then walks about the room singing softly to herself. She goes to the front-door and looks happily out into the garden. Suddenly she sees* MR. BAXTER *approaching. She hurries back into a chair and pretends to be very busy reading.*)

BAXTER (*rather nervously*). Er—may I come in, Mrs. Tremayne?

BELINDA (*dropping her book and turning round with a violent start*). Oh, Mr. Baxter, how you surprised me! (*She puts her hand to her heart.*)

BAXTER. I must apologize for intruding upon you at this hour, Mrs. Tremayne.

BELINDA (*holding up her hand*). Stop!

BAXTER (*startled*). What?

BELINDA. I cannot let you come in like that.

BAXTER (*looking down at himself*). Like what?

BELINDA (*dropping her eyes*). You called me Belinda once.

BAXTER (*coming into the room*). May I explain my position, Mrs. Tremayne?

BELINDA. Before you begin—have you seen much of my niece lately?

BAXTER (*surprised*). No.

BELINDA. Oh! (*Sweetly*) Please go on.

BAXTER. Why, is *she* lost too?

BELINDA. Oh no; I just—— Do sit down. Let me put your hat down somewhere for you.

BAXTER (*keeping it firmly in his hand, and sitting down on the sofa*). It will be all right here, thank you.

BELINDA (*returning to her chair*). I'm dying to hear what you are going to say.

BAXTER. First as regards the use of your Christian name. I felt that, as a man of honour, I could not permit myself to use it until I had established my right over that of Mr. Devenish.

BELINDA. All my friends call me Belinda.

BAXTER. As between myself and Mr. Devenish the case is somewhat different. Until one of us is successful over the other in the quest upon which you have sent us, I feel that as far as possible we should hold aloof from you.

BELINDA (*pleadingly*). Just say " Belinda " once more, in case you're a long time.

BAXTER (*very formally*). Belinda.

BELINDA. How nicely you say it—Harold.

BAXTER (*half getting out of his seat*). Mrs. Tremayne, I must not listen to this.

BELINDA (*meekly*). I won't offend again, Mr. Baxter. Please go on. Tell me about the quest; are you winning ?

BAXTER. I am progressing, Mrs. Tremayne. Indeed, I came here this morning to acquaint you with the results of my investigations. Yesterday I located a man called Robinson working upon a farm close by. I ventured to ask him if he had any marks upon him by which he could be recognized. He adopted a threatening attitude, and replied that if I wanted any he could give me some. With the aid of half a crown I managed to placate him, and was thus enabled to resume my investigations. Putting my inquiry in another form, I asked if he had any moles. A regrettable misunderstanding, which led to a fruitless journey to another part of the village, was eventually cleared up, and on my return I satisfied myself that this man was in no way related to your niece.

BELINDA (*admiringly*). How splendid of you! Well, now, we know *he's* not. (*She holds up one finger.*)

BAXTER. In the afternoon I located another Mr. Robinson following the profession of a carrier. My first inquiries led to a similar result, with the exception that in this case Mr. Robinson carried his threatening attitude so far as to take off his coat and roll up his sleeves. Perceiving at once that he was not the man, I withdrew.

BELINDA. How brave you are! That makes two. (*She holds up another finger.*) It still leaves a good many. (*Pleadingly*) Just call me Belinda again.

BAXTER (*nervously*). You mustn't tempt me, Mrs. Tremayne.

BELINDA (*penitently*). I won't!

BAXTER. To resume, then, my narrative. This morning I have heard of a third Mr. Robinson. Whether there is actually any particular fortune attached to the number three I cannot say for certain. It is doubtful whether statistics would be found to support the popular belief. But one likes to flatter oneself that in one's own case it may be true; and so——

BELINDA. And so the third Mr. Robinson——?

BAXTER. Something for which I cannot altogether account inspires me with hope. He is, I have discovered, staying at Mariton. This afternoon I go to look for him.

BELINDA (*to herself*). Mariton! How funny! I wonder if it's the same one.

BAXTER. What one?

BELINDA. Oh just one of the ones. (*Gratefully*) Mr Baxter, you are doing all this for *me*.

BAXTER. Pray do not mention it. I don't know if it's

Devonshire, or the time of the year, or the sort of atmosphere you create, Mrs. Tremayne, but I feel an entirely different man. There is something in the air which—yes, I shall certainly go over to Mariton this afternoon.

BELINDA (*gravely*). I have had the same feeling sometimes, Mr. Baxter. I am not always the staid respectable matron which I appear to you to be. Sometimes I—— (*She looks absently at the watch on her wrist*) Good gracious !

BAXTER (*alarmed*). What is it ?

BELINDA (*looking anxiously from the door to him*). Mr Baxter, I'm going to throw myself on your mercy.

BAXTER. My dear Mrs. Tremayne——

BELINDA. (*looking at her watch again*). A strange man will be here directly. He must not find you with me.

BAXTER (*rising*). A man ?

BELINDA. Yes, yes, a man ! He is pursuing me with his attentions. If he found you here, there would be a terrible scene.

BAXTER. I will defend you from him.

BELINDA. No, no. He is a big man. He will—he will overpower you.

BAXTER. But you——?

BELINDA. I can defend myself. I will send him away. But he must not find you here. You must hide before he overpowers you.

BAXTER (*with dignity*). I will withdraw if you wish it.

BELINDA. No, not withdraw, hide. He might see you withdrawing. (*Leading the way to a door on the right*) Quick, in here.

BAXTER (*embarrassed at the thought that this sort of thing really only happens in a bedroom farce*). I don't think I quite——

BELINDA (*reassuring him*). It's perfectly respectable :

it's where we keep the umbrellas. (*She takes him by the hand.*)

BAXTER (*still resisting*). I'm not at all sure that I——

BELINDA (*earnestly*). Oh, but don't you see what *trust* I'm putting in you? Some people are so nervous about their umbrellas.

BAXTER. Well, of course, if you—but I don't see why I shouldn't just slip out of the door before he comes.

BELINDA (*reproachfully*). Of course, if you grudge me every little pleasure—— Quick! Here he is.

> (*She bundles him through the door, and with a sigh of happiness comes back and looks at herself in the mirror. She goes to the front-door, waves her hand to somebody in the distance, and comes into the hall again. Seeing* MR. BAXTER's *bowler hat on the sofa, she carries it across to his door, knocks, hands it in to him, saying "Your hat. S'sh!" and returns to her chair.* TREMAYNE *comes in.*)

TREMAYNE (*at the door*). It's no good your pretending to be surprised, because you said I could come.

BELINDA (*welcoming him*). But I can still be surprised that you wanted to come.

TREMAYNE. Oh no, you aren't.

BELINDA (*marking it off on her fingers*). Just a little bit—that much.

TREMAYNE. It would be much more surprising if I hadn't come.

BELINDA (*sitting down on the sofa*). It is a pretty garden, isn't it?

TREMAYNE (*sitting down next to her*). You forget that I saw the garden yesterday.

BELINDA. Oh, but the things have grown so much since then. Let me see, this is the third day you've been and we only met three days ago.　And then you're coming to dinner again to-night.

TREMAYNE (*eagerly*).　Am I?

BELINDA.　Yes.　Haven't you been asked?

TREMAYNE.　No, not a word.

BELINDA.　Yes, that's quite right; I remember now, I only thought of it this morning, so I couldn't ask you before, could I?

TREMAYNE (*earnestly*).　What made you think of it then?

BELINDA (*romantically*).　It was at the butcher's. There was one little lamb cutlet left over and sitting out all by itself, and there was nobody to love it. And I said to myself, suddenly, " I know, that will do for Mr. Robinson."　(*Prosaically*) I do hope you like lamb?

TREMAYNE.　I adore it.

BELINDA.　Oh, I'm so glad!　When I saw it sitting there I thought you'd love it.　I'm afraid I can't tell you any more about the rest of the dinner, because I wouldn't tell Mr. Devenish, and I want to be fair.

TREMAYNE.　Who's Mr. Devenish?

BELINDA.　Oh, haven't you met him?　He's always coming here.

TREMAYNE.　Is he in love with you too?

BELINDA.　Too?　Oh, you mean Mr. Baxter.

TREMAYNE.　Confound it, that's three!

BELINDA (*innocently*).　Three?　(*She looks up at him ana down again.*)

TREMAYNE.　Who is Mr. Baxter?

BELINDA.　Oh, haven't you met him?　He's always coming here.

TREMAYNE.　Who is Mr. Baxter?

BELINDA.　Oh, he's a sort of statistician.　Isn't that a horrid word to say?　So stishany.

TREMAYNE. What does he make statistics about?

BELINDA. Oh, umbrellas and things. Don't let's talk about him.

TREMAYNE. All right, then; who is Mr. Devenish?

BELINDA. Oh, he's a poet. (*She throws up her eyes and sighs deeply.*) Ah me!

TREMAYNE. What does he write poetry about? (BELINDA *looks at him, and down again, and then at him again, and then down, and gives a little sigh—all of which means,* "Can't you guess?") What does he write poetry about?

BELINDA (*obediently*). He wrote "The Lute of Love and other Poems, by Claude Devenish." The Lute of Love—— (*To herself*) I haven't been saying that lately. (*With great expression*) The Lute of Love—the Lute. (*She pats her mouth back.*)

TREMAYNE. And what is Mr. Devenish——

BELINDA (*putting her hand on his sleeve*). You'll let me know when it's my turn, won't you?

TREMAYNE. Your turn?

BELINDA. Yes, to ask questions. I love this game—it's like clumps. (*She crosses her hands on her lap and waits for the next question.*)

TREMAYNE. I beg your pardon. I—er—ot course have no right to cross-examine you like this.

BELINDA. Oh, do go on, I love it. (*With childish excitement*) I've got my question ready.

TREMAYNE (*smiling*). I think perhaps it *is* your turn.

BELINDA (*eagerly*). Is it really? (*He nods.*) Well then—*who* is Mr. Robinson?

TREMAYNE (*alarmed*). What?

BELINDA. I think it's a fair question. I met you three days ago and you told me you were staying at Mariton. Mariton. You can say it all right now, can't you?

TREMAYNE. I think so.

BELINDA (*coaxingly*). Just say it.

TREMAYNE. Mariton.

BELINDA (*clapping her hands*). Lovely ! I don't think any of the villagers do it as well as that.

TREMAYNE. Well ?

BELINDA. Well, that was three days ago. You came the next day to see the garden, and you came the day after to see the garden, and you've come this morning —to see the garden ; and you're coming to dinner to-night, and it's so lovely, we shall simply have to go into the garden afterwards. And all I know about you is that you *haven't* any relations called Robinson.

TREMAYNE. What do I know about Mrs. Tremayne but that she *has* a relation called Robinson ?

BELINDA. And two dear friends called Devenish and Baxter.

TREMAYNE (*annoyed*). I was forgetting them.

BELINDA (*to herself*). I mustn't forget Mr. Baxter.

TREMAYNE (*getting up*). But what does it matter ? What would it matter if I knew nothing about you ? I know everything about you—everything that matters.

BELINDA (*closing her eyes contentedly*). Tell me some of them.

TREMAYNE (*earnestly*). Belinda——

BELINDA (*still with her eyes shut*). He's going to propose to me. I can feel it coming.

TREMAYNE. Confound it ! how many men *have* proposed to you ?

BELINDA (*surprised*). Since when ?

TREMAYNE. Since your first husband proposed to you.

BELINDA. Oh, I thought you meant this year. Well now, let me see. (*Slowly and thoughtfully*) One. (*She pushes up her first finger.*) Two. (*She pushes up the second.*) Three. (*She pushes up the third finger, holds it*

there for a moment and then pushes it gently down again.)
No, I don't think that one ought to count really.
(*She pushes up two more fingers and the thumb.*) Three,
four, five—do you want the names or just the total?

TREMAYNE. This is horrible.

BELINDA (*innocently*). But anybody can propose. Now
if you'd asked how many I'd accepted—— Let me
see, where was I up to? I shan't count yours, because
I haven't really had it yet. Six, seven—— Yes,
Betty, what is it?

BETTY *has just come in from the door on the left.*

BETTY. If you please, ma'am, cook would like to
speak to you for a minute.

BELINDA (*getting up*). Yes, I'll come. (*To* TREMAYNE)
You'll forgive me, won't you? You'll find some
cigarettes there. (*She starts to go, but comes back and
adds confidentially*) It's probably about the lamb cutlets;
I expect your little one refuses to be cooked.

> [*She goes out after* BETTY.
> (*Left alone,* TREMAYNE *stalks moodily about the
> room, occasionally kicking things which come in
> his way. He takes up his hat suddenly and
> goes towards the door; stops irresolutely and
> comes back. He is standing in the middle of
> the room with his hands in his pockets when*
> DEVENISH *comes in from the door on the left.*)

DEVENISH (*surprised*). Hullo!

TREMAYNE. Hullo! . . . . Are you Mr. Devenish?

DEVENISH. Yes.

TREMAYNE. Devenish the poet?

DEVENISH (*coming up and shaking him warmly by the
hand*). My dear fellow, you know my work?

TREMAYNE (*grimly*). My dear Mr. Devenish, your name
is most familiar to me.

DEVENISH. I congratulate you. I thought your great-grandchildren would be the first to hear of me.

TREMAYNE. My name's Robinson, by the way.

DEVENISH. Then let me return the compliment, Robinson. Your name is familiar to *me*.

TREMAYNE (*hastily*). I don't think I'm related to any Robinsons you know.

DEVENISH. Well, no, I suppose not. When I was very much younger I began a collection of Robinsons. Actually it was only three days ago, but it seems much longer. Many things have happened since then.

TREMAYNE (*uninterested*). Really !

DEVENISH. There is a man called Baxter who is still collecting, I believe. For myself, I am only interested in one of the great family—Delia.

TREMAYNE (*eagerly*). You are interested in *her ?*

DEVENISH. Devotedly. In fact, I am at this moment waiting for her to put on her hat.

TREMAYNE (*warmly*). My dear Devenish, I am delighted to make your acquaintance. (*He seizes his hand and grips it heartily.*) How are you?

DEVENISH (*feeling his fingers*). Fairly well, thanks.

TREMAYNE. That's right. (*They sit on the sofa together.*)

DEVENISH (*still nursing his hand*). You are a very lucky man, Robinson.

TREMAYNE. In what way ?

DEVENISH. People you meet must be so very reluctant to say good-bye to you. Have you ever tried strangling lions or anything like that ?

TREMAYNE (*with a laugh*). Well, as a matter of fact, I have.

DEVENISH. I suppose you won all right ?

TREMAYNE. In the end, with the help of my beater.

DEVENISH. Personally I should have backed you alone against any two ordinary lions.

TREMAYNE. One was quite enough. As it was, he gave me something to remember him by. (*Pulling up his left sleeve, he displays a deep scar.*)

DEVENISH (*looking at it casually*). By Jove, that's a nasty one ! (*He suddenly catches sight of the mole and stares at it fascinated.*) Good heavens !

TREMAYNE. What's the matter ?

DEVENISH (*clasping his head*). Wait. Let me think. (*After a pause*) Have you ever met a man called Baxter ?

TREMAYNE. No.

DEVENISH. Would you like to ?

TREMAYNE (*grimly*). Very much indeed.

DEVENISH. He's the man I told you about who's interested in Robinsons. He'll be delighted to meet you. (*With a nervous laugh*) Funny thing, he's rather an authority on lions. You must show him that scar of yours ; it will intrigue him immensely. (*Earnestly*) *Don't* shake hands with him too heartily just at first ; it might put him off the whole thing.

TREMAYNE. This Mr. Baxter seems to be a curious man.

DEVENISH (*absently*). Yes, he is rather odd. (*Looking at his watch*) I wonder if I—— (*To* TREMAYNE) I suppose you won't be—— (*He stops suddenly. A slight tapping noise comes from the room where they keep umbrellas.*)

TREMAYNE. What's that ?

> (*The tapping noise is repeated, a little more loudly this time.*)

DEVENISH. Come in.

> (*The door opens and* BAXTER *comes in nervously, holding his bowler-hat in his hand.*)

BAXTER. Oh, I just—(TREMAYNE *stands up*)—I just——
(*He goes back again.*)

DEVENISH (*springing across the room*). Baxter! (*The door opens nervously again and* BAXTER'S *head appears round it.*) Come in, Baxter old, man; you're just the very person I wanted. (BAXTER *comes in carefully.*) Good man. (*To* TREMAYNE) This is Mr. Baxter that I was telling you about

TREMAYNE (*much relieved at the appearance of his rival*). Oh, is this Mr. Baxter? (*Holding out his hand with great friendliness*) How are you, Mr. Baxter?

DEVENISH (*warningly*). Steady! (TREMAYNE *shakes* BAXTER *quite gently by the hand.*) Baxter, this is Mr. Robinson. (*Casually*) R-o-b-i-n-s-o-n. (*He looks sideways at* BAXTER *to see how he takes it.* BAXTER *is noticeably impressed.*)

BAXTER. Really? I am very glad to meet you, sir.

TREMAYNE. Very good of you to say so.

DEVENISH (*to* BAXTER). Robinson is a great big-game hunter.

BAXTER. Indeed? I have never done anything in that way myself, but I'm sure it must be an absorbing pursuit.

TREMAYNE. Oh, well, it's something to do.

DEVENISH (*to* BAXTER). You must get him to tell you about a wrestle he had with a lion once. Extraordinary story! (*Looking at his watch suddenly*) Jove! I must be off. See you again, Baxter. Good-bye, Robinson. No, don't shake hands. I'm in a hurry.

[*He looks at his watch again and goes out hurriedly by the door on the left.*

(TREMAYNE *and* BAXTER *sit down together on the sofa.*)

TREMAYNE. Unusual man, your friend Devenish. I suppose it comes of being a poet.

BAXTER. I have no great liking for Mr. Devenish——

TREMAYNE. Oh, he's all right.

BAXTER. But I am sure that if he is impressed by anything outside himself or his own works, it must be something rather remarkable. Pray tell me of your adventure with the lion.

TREMAYNE (*laughing*). Really, you mustn't think that I go about telling everybody my adventures. It just happened to come up. I'm afraid I shook his hand rather more warmly than I meant, and he asked me if I'd ever tried strangling lions. That was all.

BAXTER. And had you?

TREMAYNE. Well, it just happened that I had.

BAXTER. Indeed! You came off scathless, I trust?

TREMAYNE (*carelessly indicating his arm*). Well, he got me one across there.

BAXTER (*obviously excited*). Really, really. One across there. Not bad, I hope?

TREMAYNE (*laughing*). Well, it doesn't show unless I do that. (*He pulls up his sleeve carelessly and* BAXTER *bends eagerly over his arm.*)

BAXTER. Good heavens! I've found it!

TREMAYNE. Found what? (*He pulls down his sleeve.*)

BAXTER. I must see Mrs. Tremayne. Where's Mrs. Tremayne?

TREMAYNE. She went out just now. What's the matter?

BAXTER. Out! I must find her. This is a matter of life and death.

> [*He seizes his hat and hurries out by the front door.*
> (TREMAYNE *stares after him in amazement. Then he*
> *pulls up his sleeve, looks at his scar again and*
> *shakes his head. While he is still puzzling over*
> *it,* BELINDA *comes back.*)

BELINDA. Such a to-do in the kitchen! The cook's given notice—at least she will directly—and your lamb cutlet slipped back to the shop when nobody was looking, and I've got to go into the village again, and oh dear, oh dear, I have such a lot of things to do! (*Looking across at* MR. BAXTER's *door*) Oh yes, that's another one. Mr. Robinson, you will have to leave me. Farewell.

TREMAYNE. Belinda——

BELINDA. No, not even Belinda. Wait till this evening.

TREMAYNE. I have a thousand things to say to you ; I shall say them this evening.

BELINDA (*giving him her hand*). Begin about eight o'clock. Good-bye till then.

> [*He takes her hand, looks at her for a moment, then suddenly bends and kisses it, and hurries out.*
>
> (BELINDA *stands looking from her hand to him, gives a little wondering exclamation and then presses the back of her hand against her cheek. She turns back, and remembers* MR. BAXTER *again. With a smile she goes to the door and taps gently.*)

BELINDA. Mr. Baxter, Mr. Baxter, you may come in now ; he has withdrawn. I have unhanded him. (*She opens the door and finds the room empty.*) Oh !

BAXTER *comes in at the front-door.*

BAXTER. Ah, there you are !

BELINDA (*turning with a start*). Oh, how you frightened me, Mr. Baxter ! I couldn't think what had happened to you. I thought perhaps you'd been eaten up by one of the umbrellas.

BAXTER. Mrs. Tremayne, l have some wonderful news for you. I have found Miss Robinson's father.

BELINDA (*hardly understanding*). Miss Robinson's father?

BAXTER. Yes. *Mr.* Robinson.

BELINDA. Oh, you mean—— Oh yes, he told me his name was Robinson—— Oh, but he's no relation.

BAXTER. Wait! I saw his arm. By a subterfuge I managed to see his arm.

BELINDA (*her eyes opening more and more widely as she begins to realize*). You saw——

BAXTER. I saw the mole.

BELINDA (*faintly as she holds out her own arm*). Show me.

BAXTER (*very decorously indicating*). There!

> (BELINDA *holds the place with her other hand, and still looking at* MR. BAXTER, *slowly begins to laugh—half-laughter, half-tears, wonderingly, happily, contentedly.*)

BELINDA. And I didn't know!

BAXTER. Mrs. Tremayne, I am delighted to have done this service for your niece——

BELINDA (*to herself*). Of course, *he* knew all the time.

BAXTER (*to the world*). Still more am I delighted to have gained the victory over Mr. Devenish in this enterprise.

BELINDA. Eighteen years—but I *ought* to have known.

BAXTER (*at large*). I shall not be accused of exaggerating when I say that the odds against such an enterprise were enormous.

BELINDA. Eighteen years—— And now I've eight whole *hours* to wait!

BAXTER (*triumphantly*). It will be announced to-night. "Mr. Devenish," I shall say, "young fellow——" (*He arranges his speech in his mind.*)

BELINDA. So I was right, after all! He *does* look better without a beard!

BAXTER (*making his speech*). "Mr. Devenish, young fellow, when you matched yourself against a man of my repute, when you matched yourself against a man—

BELINDA *has slipped out, to enjoy her happiness alone)—*
" who has read papers at soirées of the Royal Statistical
Society ; when—er——"

> [*He looks round and discovers to his amazement that
> he is alone.　He claps on his bowler-hat, gives
> another amazed look round, says with a shrug,*
> " Unusual," *and goes out.*

ACT III

It is after dinner in BELINDA'S *hall.* BELINDA *is lying on the sofa with a coffee-cup in her hand.* DELIA, *in a chair on the right, has picked up " The Lute of Love" from a table by her side and is reading it impatiently.*

DELIA. What rubbish he writes !

BELINDA (*coming back from her thoughts*). Who, dear?

DELIA. Claude—Mr. Devenish. Of course, he's very young.

BELINDA. So was Keats, darling.

DELIA. I don't think Claude has had Keats' advantages. Keats started life as an apothecary.

BELINDA. So much nicer than a chemist.

DELIA. Now, Claude started with nothing to do.

BELINDA (*mildly*). Do you always call him Claude, darling? I hope you aren't going to grow into a flirt like that horrid Mrs. Tremayne.

DELIA. Silly mother ! (*Seriously*) I don't think he'll ever be any good till he really gets work. Did you notice his hair this evening?

BELINDA (*dreamily*). Whose, dear ?

DELIA. Mummy, look me in the eye and tell me you are not being bad.

BELINDA (*innocently*). Bad, darling ?

DELIA. You've made Mr. Robinson fall in love with you.

178

BELINDA (*happily*). Have I?

DELIA. Yes; it's serious this time.   He's not like the other two.

BELINDA. However did you know that?

DELIA. Oh, I know.

BELINDA. Darling, I believe you've grown up.   It's quite time I settled down.

DELIA. With Mr. Robinson?

   (BELINDA *looks thoughtfully at* DELIA *for a little time and then sits up.*)

BELINDA (*mysteriously*). Are you prepared for a great secret to be revealed to you?

DELIA (*childishly*). Oh, I love secrets.

BELINDA (*reproachfully*). Darling, you mustn't take it like that.   This is a great deep dark secret; you'll probably need your sal volatile.

DELIA (*excitedly*). Go on!

BELINDA. Well—— (*Looking round the room*) Shall we have the lights down a little?

DELIA. Go *on*, mummy.

BELINDA. Well, Mr. Robinson is—(*impressively*) is not quite the Robinson he appears to be.

DELIA. Yes?

BELINDA. In fact, child, he is—— Hadn't you better come over here, darling, and hold your mother's hand?

DELIA (*struggling with some emotion*). Go *on*.

BELINDA. Well, Mr. Robinson is a—sort of relation of yours; in fact (*playing with her rings*) he is your—father. (*She looks up at* DELIA *to see how the news is being received.*)   Dear one, this is not a matter for mirth.

DELIA (*coming over and kissing her*). Darling, it is lovely, isn't it?   I am laughing because I am so happy.

BELINDA. Aren't you surprised?

DELIA. No.   You see, Claude told me this morning. He found out just before Mr. Baxter.

BELINDA. Well! Everyone seems to have known except me.

DELIA. Didn't you see how friendly father and I got at dinner? I thought I'd better start breaking the ice—because I suppose he'll be kissing me directly.

BELINDA. Say you like him.

DELIA. I think he's going to be awfully nice. Does he know you know? (*She goes back to her seat.*)

BELINDA. Not yet. Just at present I've rather got Mr. Baxter on my mind. I suppose, darling, you wouldn't like him as well as Mr. Devenish? (*Pathetically*) You see, they're so used to going about together.

DELIA. Claude is quite enough.

BELINDA. I think I must see Mr. Baxter and get it over. Do you mind if I have Mr. Devenish too? I feel more at home with both of them. I'll give you him back. Oh dear, I feel so happy to-night! (*She jumps up and goes over to* DELIA.) And is my little girl going to be happy too? That's what mothers always say on the stage. I think it's so sweet.

DELIA (*smiling at her*). Yes, I think so, mummy. Of course, I'm not romantic like you. I expect I'm more like father, really.

BELINDA (*dreamily*). Jack can be romantic now. He was telling me this morning all about the people he has proposed to. I mean, I was telling *him*. Anyhow, he wasn't a bit like a father. Of course, he doesn't know he is a father yet. Darling, I think you might take him into the garden; only don't let him know who he is. You see, he ought to propose to me first, oughtn't he? (*As the men come in, she gets up.*) Here you all are! I do hope you haven't been throwing away your cigars, because smoking is allowed all over the house.

TREMAYNE. Oh, we've finished, thank you.

BELINDA. Isn't it a wonderful night?—and so warm for April. Delia, you must show Mr. Robinson the garden by moonlight—it's the only light he hasn't seen it by.

DEVENISH (*quickly*). I don't think *I've* ever seen it by moonlight, Miss Delia.

BELINDA. I thought poets were always seeing things by moonlight.

BAXTER. I was hoping, Mrs. Tremayne, that—er—perhaps——

DELIA. Come along, Mr. Robinson.

(TREMAYNE *looks at* BELINDA, *who gives him a nod.*)

TREMAYNE. It's very kind of you, Miss Robinson. I suppose there is no chance of a nightingale?

BELINDA. There ought to be. I ordered one specially for Mr. Devenish. (DELIA *and* TREMAYNE *go out together.* BELINDA *settles herself comfortably on the sofa.*) Now we're together again. Well, Mr. Devenish?

DEVENISH. Er—I——

BELINDA. No; I think I'll let Mr. Baxter speak first. I know he's longing to.

BAXTER. Yes. H'r'm! Mrs. Tremayne, I beg formally to claim your hand.

BELINDA (*sweetly*). On what grounds, Mr. Baxter?

DEVENISH (*spiritedly*). Yes, sir, on what grounds?

BAXTER. On the grounds that, as I told you this morning, I had succeeded in the quest.

DEVENISH (*appearing to be greatly surprised*). Succeeded?

BAXTER. Yes, Mr. Devenish, young fellow, you have lost. I have discovered the missing Mr. Robinson.

DEVENISH. Who—where——

BAXTER (*dramatically*). Miss Robinson has at this moment gone out with her father.

DEVENISH. Good heavens! It was he!

BELINDA (*sympathetically*). Poor Mr. Devenish!

DEVENISH (*pointing tragically to an oak settle*). And to think that I actually sat on that seat—no, not that one, it was the sofa—that I sat on the sofa with him this morning, and never guessed! Why, ten minutes ago I was asking him for the nuts!

BAXTER. Aha, Devenish, you're not so clever as you thought you were.

DEVENISH. Why, I must have given you the clue myself! He told me he had a scar on his arm, and I never thought any more of it. And then I went away innocently and left you two talking about it.

BELINDA (*alarmed*). A scar on his arm?

DEVENISH. Where a lion mauled him.

(BELINDA *gives a little shudder.*)

BAXTER. It's quite healed up now, Mrs. Tremayne.

BELINDA (*looking at him admiringly*). A lion! What you two have adventured for my sake!

BAXTER I suppose you will admit, Devenish, that I may fairly claim to have won?

(*Looking the picture of despair,* DEVENISH *droops his head, raises his arms and lets them fall hopelessly to his sides.*)

BELINDA. Mr. Devenish, I have never admired you so much as I do at this moment.

BAXTER (*indignantly to* DEVENISH). I say, you know, that's not fair. It's all very well to take your defeat like a man, but you mustn't overdo it. Mrs. Tremayne, I claim the reward which I have earned.

BELINDA (*after a pause*). Mr. Baxter—Mr. Devenish, I have something to tell you. (*Penitently*) I have not been quite frank with you. I think you both ought to know that—I—I made a mistake. Delia is not my niece; she is my daughter.

DEVENISH. Your daughter! I say, how ripping!

(BELINDA *gives him an understanding look.*)

BAXTER. Your daughter !

BELINDA. Yes.

BAXTER. But—but you aren't old enough to have a daughter of that age.

BELINDA (*apologetically*). Well, there she is.

BAXTER. But—but she's grown up.

BELINDA. Quite.

BAXTER. Then in that case you must be—— (*He hesitates, evidently working it out.*)

BELINDA (*hastily*). I'm afraid so, Mr. Baxter.

BAXTER. But this makes a great difference. I had no idea. Why, when I'm fifty you would be——

BELINDA (*sighing*). Yes, I suppose I should.

BAXTER. And when I'm sixty——

BELINDA (*pleadingly to* DEVENISH). Can't you stop him ?

DEVENISH. Look here, Baxter, another word from you and you'll never *get* to sixty.

BAXTER. And then there's Miss—er—Delia. In the event of our marrying, Mrs. Tremayne, she, I take it, would be my step-daughter.

BELINDA. I don't think she would trouble us much, Mr. Baxter. I have an idea that she will be getting married before long. (*She glances at* DEVENISH, *who returns her look gratefully.*)

BAXTER. None the less, the fact would be disturbing. I have never yet considered myself seriously as a step-father. I don't think I am going too far if I say that to some extent I have been deceived in this matter.

BELINDA (*reproachfully*). And so have I. I thought you loved me.

DEVENISH (*sympathetically*). Yes, yes.

BELINDA (*turning to him suddenly*). *And* Mr. Devenish too.

BAXTER. Er——

13

DEVENISH. Er——

(*They stand before her guiltily and have nothing to say.*)

BELINDA (*with a shrug*). Well, I shall have to marry somebody else, that's all.

BAXTER. Who?

BELINDA. I suppose Mr. Robinson. After all, if I am Delia's mother, and Mr. Baxter says that Mr. Robinson's her father, it's about time we *were* married.

DEVENISH (*eagerly*). Mrs. Tremayne, what fools we are! He *is* your husband all the time!

BELINDA. Yes.

BAXTER. You've had a husband all the time?

BELINDA (*apologetically*). I lost him; it wasn't my fault.

BAXTER. Really, this is very confusing. I don't know where I am. I gather—I am to gather, it seems, that you are no longer eligible as a possible wife?

BELINDA. I am afraid not, Mr. Baxter.

BAXTER. But this is very confusing; this is very disturbing to a man of my age. For weeks past I have been regarding myself as a—a possible benedict. I have—ah—taken steps. Only this morning, in writing to my housekeeper, I warned her that she might hear at any moment a most startling announcement.

DEVENISH (*cheerfully*). Oh, that's all right. That might only mean that you were getting a new bowler-hat.

BAXTER (*suddenly*). Ah, and what about you, sir? How is it that you take this so lightly? (*Triumphantly*) I have it. It all becomes clear to me. He has transferred his affections to your daughter!

DEVENISH. Oh, I say, Baxter, this is very crude.

BELINDA. And why should he not, Mr. Baxter? (*Softly*) He has made me very happy.

BAXTER. He has made you happy, Mrs. Tremayne?

BELINDA. Very happy.

BAXTER (*thoughtfully*). Ah! (*He takes a turn round the room in silence, and then comes back to her.*) Mrs. Tremayne, I have taken a great resolve. (*Solemnly*) I also will make you happy. (*Thumping his heart*) I also will woo Miss Delia. (*Suddenly seizing* DEVENISH'S *arm*) Come, we will seek Miss Delia together. It may be that she will send us upon another quest, in which I shall again be victorious. (*Tempestuously*) Come, I say! (*He marches the resisting* DEVENISH *towards the door.*)

DEVENISH (*to* BELINDA). Please!

BELINDA (*gently*). Mr. Baxter . . . Harold. (BAXTER *stops and turns round.*) You are too impetuous. I think that as Delia's mother——

BAXTER. Your pardon, Mrs. Tremayne. In the intoxication of the moment I am forgetting. (*Formally*) I have the honour to ask your permission to pay my addresses——

BELINDA. No, no, I didn't mean that. But, as Delia's mother, I ought to warn you that she is hardly fitted to take the place of your housekeeper. She is not very domesticated.

BAXTER (*indignantly*). Not domesticated? Why, did I not hear her tell her father at dinner that she had arranged all the flowers?

BELINDA. There are other things than flowers.

DEVENISH. Bed-socks, for instance, Baxter. It's a very tricky thing airing bed-socks. I am sure your housekeeper——

BAXTER. Mrs. Tremayne, she will learn. The daughter of such a mother . . . I need say no more.

BELINDA. Oh, thank you. But there is something else, Mr. Baxter. You are not being quite fair to yourself. In starting out upon this simultaneous wooing, you forget that Mr. Devenish has already had his turn

this morning alone. You should have yours . . . alone
. . . too.

DEVENISH. Oh, I say!

BAXTER. Yes, yes, you are right. I must introduce
myself first as a suitor. I see that. (*To* DEVENISH)
You stay here; *I* will go alone into the garden,
and——

BELINDA. It is perhaps a little cold out-of-doors for
people of . . . of *our* age, Mr. Baxter. Now, in the
library——

BAXTER (*astonished*). Library?

BELINDA. Yes.

BAXTER. You have a library?

BELINDA (*to* DEVENISH). He doesn't believe I have a
library.

DEVENISH. You ought to see the library, Baxter.

BAXTER. But you are continually springing surprises
on me this evening, Mrs. Tremayne. First a daughter,
then a husband, and then—a library! I have been
here three weeks, and I never knew you had a library.
Dear me, I wonder how it is that I never saw it?

BELINDA (*modestly*). I thought you came to see
me.

BAXTER. Yes, yes, to see you, certainly. But if I had
known you had a library. . . .

BELINDA. Oh, I am so glad I mentioned it. Wasn't it
lucky, Mr. Devenish?

BAXTER. My work has been greatly handicapped of
late by lack of certain books to which I wanted to refer.
It would be a great help——

BELINDA. My dear Mr. Baxter, my whole library is at
your disposal. (*To* DEVENISH, *as she leads the way to the
door, in a confidential whisper*) I'm just going to show him
the "Encyclopædia Britannica." You won't mind waiting—Delia will be in directly. (*She smiles at him. and*

*he opens the door for them both.   Then he goes towards the
garden door and looks outside.*)

DELIA (*from the garden*). Hullo ! we're just coming in.
     (*He goes back and waits for them.*)

TREMAYNE. Where's Mrs. Tremayne ?

DEVENISH. She's gone to the library with Baxter.

TREMAYNE (*carelessly*). Oh, the library.   Where's
that ?

DEVENISH (*promptly going towards the door and opening
it*). The end door on the right.   Right at the end.
You can't mistake it.   On the right.

TREMAYNE. Ah, yes.   (*He looks round at* DELIA.)   Yes.
(*He looks at* DEVENISH.)   Yes.   [*He goes out.*
  (DEVENISH *hastily shuts the door and comes back to*
   DELIA.)

DEVENISH. I say, your mother is a ripper.

DELIA (*enthusiastically*). Isn't she ?   (*Remembering*) At
least, you mean my aunt ?

DEVENISH (*smiling at her*). No, I mean your mother.
To think that I once had the cheek to propose to
her.

DELIA. Oh !   Is it cheek to propose to people ?

DEVENISH. To *her*.

DELIA. But not to me ?

DEVENISH. Oh, I say, Delia !

DELIA (*with great dignity*). Thank you, my name is
Miss Robinson—I mean, Tremayne.

DEVENISH. Well, if you're not quite sure which it is,
it's much safer to call you Delia.

DELIA (*smiling*). Well, perhaps it is.

DEVENISH. And if I did propose to you, you haven't
answered yet.

DELIA. If you want an answer now, it's no ; but if you
like to wait till next April——

DEVENISH (*reproachfully*). Oh, I say, and I cut my hair

for you the same afternoon. You haven't really told me how you like it yet.

DELIA. Oh, how bad of me! You look lovely.

DEVENISH. And I promised to give up poetry for your sake.

DELIA. Perhaps I oughtn't to have asked you that.

DEVENISH. As far as I'm concerned, Delia, I'll do it gladly, but, of course, one has to think about posterity.

DELIA. But you needn't be a poet. You could give posterity plenty to think about if you were a statesman.

DEVENISH. I don't quite see your objection to poetry.

DELIA. You would be about the house so much. I want you to go away every day and do great things, and then come home in the evening and tell me all about it.

DEVENISH. Then you *are* thinking of marrying me?

DELIA. Well, I was just thinking in case I had to.

DEVENISH. It would be rather fun if you did. And look here—I *will* be a statesman, if you like, and go up to Downing Street every day, and come back in the evening and tell you all about it.

DELIA. How nice of you!

DEVENISH (*magnificently, holding up a hand to Heaven*). Farewell, Parnassus!

DELIA. What does that mean?

DEVENISH. Well, it means that I've chucked poetry. A statesman's life is the life for me; behold Mr. Devenish, the new M.P.—no, look here, that was quite accidental.

DELIA (*smiling at him*). I believe I shall really like you when I get to know you.

DEVENISH. I don't know if it's you, or Devonshire, or the fact that I've had my hair cut, but I feel quite a different being from what I was three days ago.

DELIA. You *are* different. Perhaps it's your sense of humour coming back.

DEVENISH. Perhaps that's it. It's a curious feeling.

DELIA (*holding out her hand*). Let's go outside ; there's a heavenly moon.

DEVENISH (*taking her hand*). Moon ? Moon ? Now where have I heard that word before ?

DELIA. What *do* you mean ?

DEVENISH. I was trying not to be a poet. Well, I'll come with you, but I shall refuse to look at it. (*Putting his left hand behind his back, he walks slowly out with her, saying to himself*) The Prime Minister then left the House.

BELINDA *and* TREMAYNE *come in from the library.*

BELINDA (*as he opens the door*). Thank you. I don't think it's unkind to leave him, do you ? He seemed quite happy.

TREMAYNE. I shouldn't have been happy if we'd stayed.

BELINDA (*going to the sofa and putting her feet up*) Yes, but I was really thinking of Mr. Baxter.

TREMAYNE. Not of me ?

BELINDA. Well, I thought it was Mr. Baxter's turn Poor man, he's had a disappointment lately.

TREMAYNE (*eagerly*). A disappointment ?

BELINDA. Yes, he thought I was—younger than I was.

TREMAYNE (*smiling to himself*). How old are you, Belinda ?

BELINDA (*dropping her eyes*). Twenty-two. (*After a pause*) He thought I was eighteen. Such a disappointment !

TREMAYNE (*smiling openly at her*). Belinda, how old are you ?

BELINDA. Just about the right age, Mr. Robinson.

TREMAYNE. The right age for what?

BELINDA. For this sort of conversation.

TREMAYNE. Shall I tell you how old you are?

BELINDA. Do you mean in figures or—poetically?

TREMAYNE. I meant——

BELINDA. Mr. Devenish said I was as old as the—now, I must get this the right way round—as old as the——

TREMAYNE. I don't want to talk about Mr. Devenish.

BELINDA (*with a sigh*). Nobody ever does—except Mr. Devenish. As old as the stars, and as young as the dawn. (*Settling herself cosily*) I think that's rather a nice age to be, don't you?

TREMAYNE. A very nice age to be.

BELINDA. It's a pity he's thrown me over for Delia; I shall miss that sort of thing rather. You don't say those sort of things about your aunt-in-law—not so often.

TREMAYNE (*eagerly*). He really is in love with Miss Robinson?

BELINDA. Oh yes. I expect he is out in the moonlight with her now, comparing her to Diana.

TREMAYNE. Well, that accounts for *him*. Now what about Baxter?

BELINDA. I thought I told you. Deeply disappointed to find that I was four years older than he expected, Mr. Baxter hurried from the drawing-room and buried himself in a column of the "Encyclopædia Britannica."

TREMAYNE. Well, that settles Baxter. Are there any more men in the neighbourhood?

BELINDA (*shaking her head*). Isn't it awful? I've only had those two for the last three weeks.

> (TREMAYNE *sits on the back of the sofa and looks down at her.*)

TREMAYNE. Belinda.

BELINDA. Yes, Henry ?

TREMAYNE. My name is John.

BELINDA. Well, you never told me. I had to guess. Everybody thinks they can call me Belinda without giving me the least idea what their own names are. You were saying, John ?

TREMAYNE. My friends call me Jack.

BELINDA. Jack Robinson. That's the man who always goes away so quickly. I hope you're making more of a stay ?

TREMAYNE. Oh, you maddening, maddening woman !

BELINDA. Well, I have to keep the conversation going. You do nothing but say " Belinda."

TREMAYNE (*taking her hand*). Have you ever loved anybody seriously, Belinda ?

BELINDA. I don't ever do anything very seriously. The late Mr. Tremayne, my first husband—Jack—— Isn't it funny, *his* name was Jack—he used to complain about it too sometimes.

TREMAYNE (*with conviction*). Silly ass !

BELINDA. I think you are a little hard on the late Mr. Tremayne.

TREMAYNE. Has he been dead long ?

BELINDA. Dead to me.

TREMAYNE. You quarrelled ?

BELINDA. Yes. It was his fault entirely.

TREMAYNE. I'm sure it was.

BELINDA. How sweet of you to say that !

TREMAYNE. Belinda, I want you to marry me and forget about him.

BELINDA (*happily to herself*). This is the proposal that those lamb cutlets interrupted this morning.

TREMAYNE. Belinda, I love you—do you understand ?

BELINDA. Suppose my first husband turns up suddenly like—like E. A. ?

TREMAYNE. Like who?

BELINDA. Well, like anybody.

TREMAYNE. He won't—I know he won't. Don't you love me enough to risk it, Belinda?

BELINDA. I haven't really said I love you at all yet.

TREMAYNE. Well, say it now. (BELINDA *looks at him, and then down again.*) You do! Well, I'm going to have a kiss, anyway. (*He comes round the sofa and kisses her quickly.*) There!

BELINDA. O-oh! The late Mr. Tremayne never did that.

TREMAYNE. I have already told you that he was a silly ass. (*Sitting down on the sofa*) Belinda——

BELINDA. Yes, Henry—I mean, Jack?

TREMAYNE. Do you know who I am? (*He is thoroughly enjoying the surprise he is about to give her.*)

BELINDA (*nodding*). Yes, Jack.

TREMAYNE. Who?

BELINDA. Jack Tremayne.

TREMAYNE (*jumping up*). Good heavens, you *know!*

BELINDA (*gently*). Yes, Jack.

TREMAYNE (*angrily*). You've known all the time that I was your husband, and you've been playing with me and leading me on?

BELINDA (*mildly*). Well, darling, you knew all the time that I was your wife, and you've been making love to me and leading me on.

TREMAYNE. That's different.

BELINDA. That's *just* what the late Mr. Tremayne said, and then he slammed the door and went straight off to the Rocky Mountains and shot bears; and I didn't see him again for eighteen years.

TREMAYNE (*remorsefully*). Darling, I was a fool then, and I'm a fool now.

BELINDA. I was a fool then, but I'm not such a fool

now—I'm not going to let you go. It's quite time I married and settled down.

TREMAYNE. You darling! How did you find out who I was?

BELINDA (*awkwardly*). Well, it was rather curious, darling. (*After a pause*) It was April, and I felt all sort of Aprily, and—and—there was the garden all full of daffodils—and—and there was Mr. Baxter—the one we left in the library—knowing all about moles. He's probably got the M volume down now. Well, we were talking about them one day, and I happened to say that the late Mr. Tremayne—that was you, darling—had rather a peculiar one on his arm. And then he happened to see it this morning and told me about it.

TREMAYNE. What an extraordinary story!

BELINDA. Yes, darling; it's really much more extraordinary than that. I think perhaps I'd better tell you the rest of it another time. (*Coaxingly*) Now show me where the nasty lion scratched you. (TREMAYNE *pulls up his sleeve.*) Oh! (*She kisses his arm.*) You shouldn't have left Chelsea, darling.

TREMAYNE. I should never have found you if I hadn't.

BELINDA (*squeezing his arm*). No, Jack, you wouldn't. (*After a pause*) I—I've got another little surprise for you if—if you're ready for it. (*Standing up*) Properly speaking, I ought to be wearing white. I shall certainly stand up while I'm telling you. (*Modestly*) Darling, we have a daughter—our little Delia.

TREMAYNE. Delia? You said her name was Robinson.

BELINDA. Yes, darling, but you said yours was. One always takes one's father's name. Unless, of course, you were Lord Robinson.

TREMAYNE. But you said her name was Robinson

before you—oh, never mind about that. A daughter! Belinda, how could you let me go and not tell me?

BELINDA. You forget how you'd slammed the door. It isn't the sort of thing you shout through the window to a man on his way to America.

TREMAYNE (*taking her in his arms*). Oh, Belinda, don't let me ever go away again.

BELINDA. I'm not going to, Jack. I'm going to settle down into a staid old married woman.

TREMAYNE. Oh no, you're not. You're going on just as you did before. And I'm going to propose to you every April, and win you, over all the other men in love with you.

BELINDA. You darling!

DELIA *and* DEVENISH *come in from the garden.*

TREMAYNE (*quietly to* BELINDA). Our daughter.

DELIA (*going up to* TREMAYNE). You're my father.

TREMAYNE. If you don't mind very much, Delia.

DELIA. You've been away a long time.

TREMAYNE. I'll do my best to make up for it.

BELINDA. Delia, darling, I think you might kiss your poor old father.

(*As she does so,* DEVENISH *suddenly and hastily kisses* BELINDA *on the cheek.*)

DEVENISH. Just in case you're going to be my mother-in-law.

TREMAYNE. We seem to be rather a family party.

BELINDA (*suddenly*). There! We've forgotten Mr Baxter again.

BAXTER (*who has come in quietly with a book in his hand*). Oh, don't mind about me, Mrs. Tremayne. I've enjoyed myself immensely. (*Referring to his book*) I have been collecting some most valuable information on (*looking up at them*) lunacy in the—er—county of *Devonshire.*

THE RED FEATHERS

AN OPERETTA IN ONE ACT

THE RED FEATHERS

*In the living-room of a country-house, half farm, half
manor, a* MOTHER *and her* DAUGHTER *are sitting. It
is any year you please—between, let us say, the day
when the fiddle first came to England and the day when
Romance left it. As for the time of the year, let us
call it May. Oh yes, it is certainly May, and about
twelve o'clock, and the* DAUGHTER *is singing at the
spinet, while her* MOTHER *is at her needlework.
Through the lattice windows the murmur of a stream
can be heard, on whose banks—but we shall come to that
directly. Let us listen now to what the* DAUGHTER *is
singing :*

Life passes by.
I do not know its pleasure or its pain—
The Spring was here, the Spring is here again,
        The Spring will die.

Life passes by.
The doors of Pain and Pleasure open wide,
The crowd streams in—and I am left outside. . . .
        They know ; not I.

You don't like it ? Neither did her Mother.

MOTHER (*looking up from her work*). Yes, I should call
that a melancholy song, dear.

DAUGHTER. It is sung by a melancholy person,
Mother.

197

MOTHER. Why are you that, child?

DAUGHTER (*getting up*). I want so much that I shall never have.

MOTHER. Well, so do we all.

DAUGHTER (*impatiently*). Oh, why does nothing ever happen? We sit here all day, and we sing or do our embroidery, and we go to bed, and the next day we get up and do the same things over again, and so it goes on. Mother, is that all there is in the world?

MOTHER. It's all there is in our world.

DAUGHTER. Are we so very poor?

MOTHER. We have the house—and very little else.

DAUGHTER. Oh, I wish that we were *really* poor——

MOTHER. You needn't wish, child.

DAUGHTER. Oh, but I mean so that it wouldn't matter what clothes we wore; so that we could wander over the hills and down into the valleys, and sleep perhaps in a barn and bathe ourselves in the brook next morning, and——

MOTHER. I don't think I should like that very much. Perhaps I'm peculiar.

DAUGHTER. Oh, if only I were a boy to go out and make my own way in the world. Would you let me go, Mother, if I were a boy?

MOTHER. I don't suppose you'd ask me, dear.

DAUGHTER (*sighing*). Oh, well! We must make the best of it, I suppose. Perhaps one day something will happen. (*She goes back to the spinet and sings again.*)

> *Lads and lasses, what will you sell,*
> *What will you sell?*

Four stout walls and a roof atop,
   Warm fires gleaming brightly,
Well-stored cellar and garnered crop,
   Money-bags packed tightly;

An ordered task in an ordered day,
    And a sure bed nightly ;
Years which peacefully pass away,
    Until Death comes lightly.

Lads and lasses, what will you buy ?
    What will you buy ?

Here is a cap to cover your head,
    A cap with one red feather ;
Here is a cloak to make your bed
    Warm or winter weather ;
Here is a satchel to store your ware,
    Strongly lined with leather ;
And here is a staff to take you there
    When you go forth together.

Lads and lasses, what will you gain,
    What will you gain ?

Chatter of rooks on tall elm-trees
    New Spring houses taking ;
Daffodils in an April breeze
    Golden curtsies making ;
Shadows of clouds across the weald
    From hill to valley breaking,
The first faint stir which the woodlands yield
    When the world is waking.

Lads and lasses, this is your gain,
    This is your gain.

(*Towards the end of the song the face and shoulders of the
    *TALKER *appear at the open lattice window on the left.
    He listens with a bland and happy smile until the song
    is finished.*)

    TALKER. Brava ! Brava ! (*They turn round towards
the window in astonishment.*) A vastly pleasing song,

vastly well sung. Mademoiselle Nightingale, permit me to felicitate you. (*Turning to the Mother*) The Mother of the Nightingale also. Mon Dieu, what a voice, of a richness, of a purity! To live with it always! Madame, I felicitate you again.

MOTHER. I must ask you, sir, to explain the meaning of this intrusion.

TALKER. Intrusion? Oh, fie! Madame, not intrusion. My feet stand upon the highway. The road, Madame, is common to all. I can quote you Rex—— What does Rex, cap. 27, para. 198, say? *Via*, says Rex, meaning the road; *communis* is common; *omnibus* to all, meaning thereby—but perchance I weary you?

DAUGHTER. Mother, who is he?

TALKER. Ah, Mademoiselle Nightingale, you may indeed ask. Who is he? Is he the Pope of Rome? Nay, he is not the Pope of Rome. Is he the Cham of Tartary? Nay, he is not the Cham of Tartary, for an he were the Cham of Tartary——

MOTHER. I beg you, sir, to tell us as shortly as you can who you are and what you want.

TALKER. Madam, by nature I am a taciturn man; Silent John I am named by my friends. I am a glum body, a reserved creature. These things you will have already noticed. But now I will commit to you a secret, known only to my dearest friends. Uncommunicative as I am by nature (*he disappears and reappears at the middle window*), I am still more so when compelled to hold converse with two such ornaments of their sex (*he disappears and reappears at the right-hand window*) through a lattice window. Am I getting any nearer the door?

MOTHER (*resigned*). Pray, sir, come in and tell us all about it. I see that we must have your tale.

TALKER. To be exact, Madame, I have two tails who

follow me about everywhere. One is of my own poor sex, a man, a thing of whiskers ; the other has the honour to belong to that sex which—have I said it ?— you and Mademoiselle so adorn. Have I your ladyship's permission ?

DAUGHTER (*eagerly*). Oh, Mother, let them come.

MOTHER. Well, I suppose I must have you all.

TALKER (*with a bow*). Madame, I shall never forget this. Though I live to be ninety-three, this will always be engraved upon my memory. My grandchildren climbing upon my knee will wonder sometimes of what the old man is thinking. Little will they know——— But I will attend you further within.

[*He bows and disappears.*

DAUGHTER. Mother, something *is* going to happen at last.

MOTHER. Oh, child, were you as weary as that ?

The TALKER *comes in at the door, followed by the* SINGER *and the* FIDDLER. *The* SINGER *is a pleasant-looking man of middle height, the* FIDDLER *a tall, silent girl. The* TALKER *himself is short and round, with a twinkling eye. Each wears a cap with a red feather in it.*

TALKER. Madame, your humble and most devoted servants. I have the honour to present to you her Royal Sweetness the Princess Carissima, His Flutiness the Duke of Bogota, and myself a mere Marquis.

DAUGHTER. Oh, Mother, they're wandering minstrels.

MOTHER. I bid you all welcome, sir.

TALKER. Permit me to expound further. The Princess —a courtesy title bestowed by myself last Michaelmas Day—plays upon the fiddle with an unerring beauty which makes strong men weep. You shall hear her.

I pray you have your handkerchers ready. His Flutiness the Duke—the title was granted last Candlemas—
has a voice of a rare richness. He is cursed with a
melancholy disposition most pleasing. He suffers from
a surfeit of rejected love. A most waggish companion
withal.

DAUGHTER. Oh, what a shame !

SINGER. You must not believe all that Johannes says,
ladies.

MOTHER. I had already learnt that much, sir.

TALKER. For myself, I play upon the pipe. You shall
hear. (*He plays " cuckoo" with an air.*)

SINGER. The only notes he knows, ladies.

TALKER (*indignantly*). Oh, fie, sir, fie ! I protest,
Madame, he maligns me. Have I not a G of surpass-
ing splendour, of a fruitiness rarely encountered in this
vale of tears? Madame, you must hear my G. Now
where is it? (*He arranges his fingers with great care on
the pipe.*) I have it. (*He blows a G, and bows deeply
first to* MOTHER *and then to* DAUGHTER.)

SINGER. Marvellous !

MOTHER (*to* TALKER). I thank you, sir.

DAUGHTER. Oh, Mother, isn't he splendid?

TALKER (*to* MOTHER). Would you like my G again,
Madame ?

MOTHER. Not just now, I thank you, sir. Doubtless
we shall feel more in need of it a little later on. But
tell me, sir, have you no other talent to match the
singing and playing of your friends?

FIDDLER. He talks.

MOTHER. I had noticed it.

TALKER. This gift of talking with which her Royal
Sweetness is good enough to credit me, irksome though
it is to a man of silent habit like myself, a creature, as
you will have noticed, of taciturn disposition; this—

I——— (*Frankly*) Madame, I have lost that sentence. Have I your gracious permission to begin again?

MOTHER. I think it would be better, sir.

TALKER. Then, to put it shortly, Madame———

MOTHER. If you could, sir.

TALKER. To be completely frank in this matter, Madame, I—er—go round with the hat. It is a sordid but necessary business.

DAUGHTER (*eagerly*). Oh, I hope they give you plenty of money.

TALKER. Enough to support life, Mademoiselle. The hungry look which you observe upon His Flutiness is, as I have explained, due to melancholy.

DAUGHTER. You are going to perform, aren't you?

TALKER. Of a surety, Mademoiselle. Perhaps I should add that for myself I am resting just now, and that my part of the performance will be limited to nothing more than a note or two upon the pipe.

MOTHER (*with a friendly smile*). Sir, you are generous. We shall be glad to hear your friends.

(*The* TALKER *bows and turns to his company.*)

TALKER. A song, good Master Duke, a song which her Royal Sweetness will accompany upon the fiddle. Let it end, I pray you, with a G, so that I may bring the thing to a climax upon the last note.

FIDDLER (*to* SINGER). Morland Hill.

SINGER. You like that? (*She nods.*)   Very well. (*He sings.*)

> Oh, when the wind is in the North,
> I take my staff and sally forth;
> And when it whistles from the East
> I do not mind it in the least;
> The warm wind murmurs through the trees
> Its messages from Southern seas;

But after all perhaps the best
Is that which whispers from the West.

> Oh let the wind, the wind be what it will,
> So long as I may walk on Morland Hill!

The staff which helps to carry me,
I cut it from the Hazel-tree;
But once I had a cudgel torn
Most circumspectly from the Thorn;
I know a fellow, far from rash,
Who swears entirely by the Ash;
And all good travellers invoke
A blessing on the mighty Oak.

> Oh let the wood, the wood be what it will,
> So long as I may walk on Morland Hill!

Some years ago I gave my heart
To Prue until we had to part;
Then, seeing Susan's pretty face,
I left it with her for a space;
And Susan had my heart until
I wanted it for Mistress Jill;
I think, although I am not clear,
That Chloe's had it this last year.

> Oh let the wench, the wench be whom you will,
> So long as I may walk on Morland Hill!

(*The* TALKER *comes in proudly on the last note and takes most of the applause.*)

DAUGHTER. I'm not sure that I like that last verse.

TALKER. Oh, you mustn't believe all he sings. A cursed melancholy fellow by nature. But waggish— waggish withal.

SINGER (*to* DAUGHTER). We have to sing what the

poets write for us, Mademoiselle. Had I written a song myself, it had been about one woman only.

TALKER. And there would have been a hundred and twenty-five verses to it.

MOTHER. Your song was well sung, sir; I thank you for it. (*To the* FIDDLER) Will you not play us something now?

FIDDLER. If you wish it.

TALKER. You would wish me to accompany her, of course.

MOTHER (*with a smile*). It is kind of you, sir, but I think perhaps my daughter——

DAUGHTER (*eagerly*). Yes, of course, I will if I can. (*She goes to the spinet.*)

FIDDLER (*playing a few notes*). Do you know this?

DAUGHTER. Yes, I think so. (*She plays. At the end of it the* TALKER *finds himself bowing to the applause.*)

TALKER. And now, Madame, you have had a sample of all our poor talents, save and except that paltry talent of mine which in other company concludes such a performance. I pray you tell me what you think of the entertainment.

MOTHER. I have enjoyed it immensely, good Master Johannes. And if you did wish to exercise that talent of yours, of which so far we have only heard——

TALKER. Nay, nay, Madame, I beg you.

MOTHER. Then, sir, I offer you my grateful thanks for your entertainment.

DAUGHTER. And I too.

TALKER. Ladies, you are too kind—er—(*he hesitates*) —er——

MOTHER. Yes?

TALKER. The fact is, Madame, that now we approach or, so to speak, draw nigh or adjacent—in other words, Madame, we are perilously approximate—— –

FIDDLER. Tell her straight out.

MOTHER. Tell her what?

FIDDLER. What we've come for.

SINGER. Master Johannes, Madam, is so accustomed when he goes round with the hat to disguise under a flow of words the fact that money is as necessary to an artist as applause, that he has lost the habit of saying anything in less than ten sentences.

TALKER (*mournfully*). And yet I am a taciturn man.

MOTHER. Well, will somebody tell me, for I confess I have been wondering what is behind it all.

FIDDLER. Tell her, Johannes.

TALKER. If you will allow me, Madame. But tell me first, did you notice anything lacking in our performance?

MOTHER (*surprised*). No; I don't think so.

TALKER (*to* DAUGHTER). Perhaps you, Mademoiselle?

DAUGHTER (*shyly*). It seemed to lack a woman's voice, sir.

TALKER (*admiringly*). What intelligence! What profundity! (*To* MOTHER) Madam, I felicitate you again on your daughter. Unerringly she has laid her finger on the weak joint in our armour. We have no woman's voice.

MOTHER. Well, sir, I don't see how I can help you.

TALKER. Madame, you have a nightingale. It has lived in a cage all its life. It looks through the bars sometimes, and sees the great world outside, and sighs and turns back to its business of singing. Madame, it would sing better outside in the open air, with the other birds.

MOTHER. I don't understand you, sir. Are you referring to my daughter?

TALKER (*looking towards the window*). There is a stream which runs beyond the road, with a green bank to it.

We were seated on that bank, I and my two companions, eating our bread and cheese, and washing it down with draughts from that good stream. We were tired, for we had come from over the hills that morning, and it was good to lie on our backs there and watch the little clouds taking shape after shape in the blue, and so to dream our dreams. In a little while the road would take us westward, here through a wood banked with primroses, there across a common or between high spring hedges with the little stream babbling ever at the side of us. And in the evening we would come to an inn, where there would be good company, and we would sing and play to them, and they would reward us. (*With a shrug*) It is a pleasant life.

DAUGHTER (*eagerly*). Oh, go on!

MOTHER. Yes, go on, sir.

TALKER. We were lying on our backs thus, Madame, when we heard the nightingale. " Duke," says I, " it is early yet for the nightingale." His Flutiness removes his cap from his face, takes a squint at the sun, and says " Monstrous early, good Master Johannes," and claps his cap back again. " What says you, Fiddler," says I, " in this matter of nightingales? Is it possible," says I ; " the sun being where it is, and nightingales being what they are—to wit, nightingales?" " It's not a nightingale," says Fiddler dreamily, " it's a girl." " Then," says I, jumping up, " it is a girl we want. She must put the red feather in her cap, and come her ways with us." (*With a bow*) Madame, your humble servant.

DAUGHTER. Oh, Mother, you will let me go, won't you? I must, I must! He is quite right. I'm caged here. Oh, you will let me see something of the world before I grow old!

FIDDLER (*suddenly*). Yes, let her come. If she feels like that, she ought to come.

SINGER (*with a very winning smile*). We will take great care of her, Madame, as if she were our own sister.

MOTHER (*surprisingly to* JOHANNES). What do you think of cider as a drink, Master Johannes ?

TALKER (*who had not expected it, but is always ready*). Cider—ah, there's a drink ! Oh, I can talk to you about cider, glum body as I am by nature, having been as it were taciturn from birth. Yet of cider I could talk you——

MOTHER. Ours is considered very good cider. (*To her daughter*) Take them, child, and give them such refreshment as they want. They have deserved it for their entertainment.

DAUGHTER. Why, of course, Mother. Come this way please.

> [*She leads the way, and the others follow, the* TALKER *coming last and murmuring " Cider " to himself.*

MOTHER. Master Johannes. (*He turns round.*) A word with you, if you please, sir.

TALKER. But certainly, Madame. The cider will be all the better for the expectation.

MOTHER. Sit down, please. (*He does so.*) Master Johannes, who are you, all of you ?

TALKER. I thought I had explained, Madame. Her Royal Sweetness Princess Carissima, His Flutiness the Duke of Bogota, and myself a humble Marquis. We may be referred to collectively as the Red Feathers For myself I am sometimes called Silent John, being of a close disposition.

MOTHER. Whatever you are called, you are, I think, a man of the world, and you will understand that if I am

to trust my daughter to you, for however little a time,
I must know something more about you.

TALKER. Madame, I will make a confession to you,
a confession I have never yet made to man, woman, or
child. I am forty-six years of age ; it is, in fact, my
birthday. Were I to begin to tell you something about
myself, starting from that day, forty-six years ago, when
I was born—were I to begin—well, Madame, I am
only too ready to begin. It is a subject I find vastly
pleasant. But, (*looking at her comically*) shall I begin ?

MOTHER (*with a smile*). Would you make it so long
a story, sir ?

TALKER (*with a sigh*). The tongue is an unruly member,
and to one who has but three notes on the pipe, and
yet desires to express himself, talking is a great comfort.

MOTHER. I said you were a man of the world, sir.
May I say now that I think you must be a man of *our*
world ?

TALKER. I am a man of many worlds. But if it would
comfort your mother's heart to know that your daughter
will be in good company, I think I can give you that
comfort.

MOTHER. Is that all you can give me ?

> (*The* TALKER *gets up and walks about, frowning to
> himself. Suddenly he takes out his pipe, plays
> "cuckoo" to himself very solemnly, and is
> immensely relieved thereby. He comes back to
> the* MOTHER *with a beaming face.*)

TALKER. Madame, I will tell you a story. (*Holding
up his hand to stop any expostulation*) No, quite a short
one. Once on a time there was a certain noble gentleman, a baron of estates and family. Conceiving himself to be in love, he dared to put it to the touch to win
or lose it all. I regret to say that he lost it all. In a
fit of melancholy he abjured society, cursed all women

and took to the road. A pleasant melancholy gentleman. I made him a duke.

MOTHER (*eagerly, indicating the door out of which the duke has just gone*). You mean he really is——

TALKER. We will name no names, madame. I doubt not I have no right to speak of him to another. It is just a story. (*Putting his pipe to his lips*) Cuck-oo!

MOTHER. Poor child, she is not happy here. We live so quietly; we have no neighbours. I have wondered what to do—it seemed that I could do so little. If only I could be sure—— (*Suddenly*) Master Johannes, do you like the look of this house with its little stream opposite, and the green bank running down, on which one may lie on one's back and look up at the sky?

TALKER. Did we not single it out above all others by having our bread and cheese outside it?

MOTHER. Will you all stay with me for a little? I think I can find room for you. Before I can lend my daughter to you, I feel that I must know something of you. I think that is the best way, is it not? (*With a very friendly smile*) The cider is good, you know.

TALKER (*rising and bowing*). Madame, we need say no more.

The other three come in. The DAUGHTER *has found from somewhere a cap with a red feather in it. They stand in a row opposite the* MOTHER, *and to the* FIDDLER'S *accompaniment sing a merry song.*

TOGETHER.   The cuckoo comes in April,
                        Sings his song in May,
                    Changes his tune in the middle of June,
                        And then he flies away.

HE.   The cuckoo comes when April's here—
                    He is not very good, I fear.

> He goes and takes another nest—
> Perhaps he does it for the best.
> > Cuckoo ! Cuckoo ! . . .

SHE

> When April's over he begins
> Repenting of his former sins ;
> From tree to tree he takes his way,
> But this is all he finds to say :
> > Cuckoo ! Cuckoo ! . . .

HE.

> By June he gets a trifle flat,
> Which is not to be wondered at,
> And critical observers note
> A huskiness about the throat.
> > (*Huskily*) Cuckoo ! Cuckoo ! . . .

SHE.

> Alas ! he does not stay for long,
> But other birds take up the song
> Of summer gently following
> The wild and happy days of Spring.
> > Cuckoo !

(The TALKER *conducts with his pipe in his hand, and hums " La, la, la !" to himself. He pipes the chorus with them. At the conclusion they all bow or curtsey deeply to the* MOTHER.*)*

MOTHER (*half laughing, half crying*). Oh !

TALKER (*suddenly and dramatically, holding up his hand*). Listen !

EVERYBODY. What ?

TALKER. Didn't I hear somebody say " cider " ?

    *   *   *   *   *

(It is eight days later when we see them again. The DAUGHTER *is at the spinet, playing an accompaniment to the song which she and the* SINGER *are sharing for the moment.)*

SHE.

He does not know I love him,
    He does not care ;
The sky is blue above him,
    The road is there
    For those who dare—
    Alas ! why should he care ?

HE.

She does not know I love her,
    She does not know ;
The sky is blue above her,
    The soft winds blow
    Where violets grow—
    Alas ! how should she know ?

TOGETHER.

Yet those who sing
About the Spring
All say it should bring
    Two lovers together !
Oh where, oh where
Will you find a pair
    So matched as you and I, love ?
Come rain or shine,
Come wet or fine,
If you are mine
    What matter the weather ?
Oh take my hand
And kiss me and
    Confess that you are my love.

HE.

She does not know I love her—
    Ah yes, she knows ;
The sky is blue above her,
    The buds disclose
    The first wild rose—
Ah yes, she knows, she knows !

SHE.
> He cares not that I love him—
>> Ah yes, he cares;
> The sky is blue above him,
>> A thrush declares
>> The world is theirs—
> Ah yes, how much he cares!

TOGETHER. For those who sing, etc.

DAUGHTER (*looking up at him*). It is a pretty song.

SINGER. The words, I thought, were good. I liked the words.

DAUGHTER. Who thinks of the words of a song if the tune be pretty?

SINGER. But if the heart of the singer be in the words?

DAUGHTER (*suddenly, as she gets up*). Tell me about Chloe.

SINGER (*surprised*). Chloe?

DAUGHTER. Or whatever her name was.

SINGER (*hurt*). I am not sure that I understand this conversation.

DAUGHTER. I mean the first one.

SINGER. I am not sure that I like this conversation.

DAUGHTER. She was the first, wasn't she—the one who made you renounce the world and take to the road?

SINGER (*stiffly*). Her name was not Chloe.

DAUGHTER (*coaxingly*). What was it?

SINGER (*annoyed*). Why rake up the dead ashes of the past? I was but a boy. It was five months ago. Besides, her name was Penelope.

DAUGHTER. You still remember it, though it was so long ago?

SINGER. I could have pretended to have forgotten, if it would have pleased you better.

DAUGHTER (*coldly*). I? Oh, I am not interested.

SINGER. Well, *I* didn't start the subject. Perhaps, as neither of us is interested, I had better withdraw. Since we are to start this afternoon, I have much to see about. (*Bowing*) With your permission.

DAUGHTER (*stopping him*). Don't go. I am sorry. I have been unkind.

SINGER (*smiling*). Shall we practise that other song? Our voices agree, if our—our hearts do not.

DAUGHTER (*distressed*). Oh, don't say that. We must be friends.

SINGER. Only friends?

DAUGHTER (*gently*). Tell me about her.

SINGER. There is not much to tell, dear. I thought she loved me. Perhaps that was why I thought I loved *her*. When I told her, she pretended to be surprised. I don't think she was surprised. She was very pretty. (*He pauses.*)

DAUGHTER. And hard?

SINGER. It is not for me to say anything against her. It is through her that I came here.

DAUGHTER. When you came here the other day, had you forgotten her?

SINGER (*singing*). " Oh, let the wench, the wench be whom she will, so long as I can walk on Morland Hill." Didn't I say so on that first day?

DAUGHTER. Of course, I know very little of the world, but I do wonder sometimes if people who sing about the joys of wandering *are* really enjoying it all the time.

SINGER (*looking round at the window*). Is Johannes about?

DAUGHTER (*surprised*). No.

SINGER. Then I will be frank with you. Just lately *I* have been wondering too.

DAUGHTER. Oh !

SINGER (*rapidly*). I have a house ; you would like my house. I have a park : you would like the park. Horses to ride and jewels to wear. I go to London sometimes and see the King ; you would like London.

DAUGHTER (*tragically*). I have never been to London.

SINGER (*letting himself go suddenly*). Sweetheart, all that I have—— (*In an ordinary whisper*) Be careful, Fiddler just went past the window. (*Keeping his arm round her, he breaks into the last line or two of his song. She joins in, as if they were rehearsing.*)

Enter the FIDDLER.

SINGER (*to* DAUGHTER). Yes, I think we have it pretty well now. 'Tis a good song. (*Turning round suddenly and seeing the* FIDDLER). Ah, Fiddler, are you there ? What do you think of it ?

FIDDLER. Isn't it time to start ?

SINGER. To start ? Ah yes, we start this afternoon. Well, we have had a pleasant holiday and must get to work again.

DAUGHTER (*eagerly*). And I am coming with you.

FIDDLER. It is settled ?

DAUGHTER. Oh yes, I think so.

FIDDLER. It is the best life. (*To* DAUGHTER) Play something.

> [*As the* DAUGHTER *goes to the spinet, the* SINGER *goes out.*
>
> (*They play. When it is over, the* DAUGHTER *turns round and looks at the* FIDDLER, *and sighs.*)

DAUGHTER. That is all you want ? Just you and your fiddle and the open road ?

FIDDLER. It is the best life.

15

The TALKER *appears at the window.*

TALKER. Aha! what did I hear? Did I hear our ˌoquacious Fiddler perorating upon Life? "Life," quoth she, with much argument and circumstantial matter; "Life," she continued, making her points singly and one by one, thus keeping the business in its true perspective; "Life is——" (*Lamely*) Well, what is life?

FIDDLER. When do we start, Johannes?

[*The* DAUGHTER *goes out.*

TALKER. Are you so eager to be gone?

FIDDLER. We have been here eight days.

TALKER. Eight days! And Troy was besieged for eleven years! Eight days! Why, I could talk for eight days without taking breath, and I am by nature a glum, silent man. Nay, nay, say not to me "Eight days." Eight days will not make a man grow old or a woman lose her beauty. (*The* MOTHER *comes into the room.*) Or a woman lose her beauty—Madame, I kiss your hands. Were I of less girth I would flit through the window and fall upon my knees at your feet. (*The* FIDDLER *with a shrug goes out.*) As it is, I shall enter by the door in the usual way. I have your permission?

MOTHER (*smiling*). You asked my permission a week ago. You do not need to ask it now.

TALKER (*still at the window*). It has been a happy week. The week has liked me well.

MOTHER. You take the road again this afternoon Your plan still holds?

TALKER (*with a sigh*). They say so, lady.

MOTHER. Who say so? Is not Master Jonannes the master of his company? Who say so?

TALKER. The birds. I held converse with a cuckoo-bird this morning. "Cuckoo," he said—in this manner (*he imitates it on his pipe*)—meaning, as I gathered, "O fool!" I bowed low to him, and "Pardon, bird," said I, "but I would have you tell me why I am a fool." He answered thus in parables—"Cuckoo."

MOTHER. And what did *that* mean?

TALKER (*sighing*). It meant, "There's no fool like an old fool.'

> (*She looks away. He waits a little, then sighs again and leaves the window, entering a moment later by the door.*

MOTHER (*looking up*). Well, sir?

TALKER. Madame, I am a man of good family, although—although I quarrelled with my good family. I left them many years ago and took to the road. I have seen something of the world since then, but I think I must always have had at the back of my mind some dim picture of what a home was—some ancient memory, perhaps. That memory has been very strong within me these last days.

MOTHER. You have liked my home, Master Johannes?

TALKER. I have liked it well. (*He takes out his pipe and plays a melancholy "Cuckoo."*) Well, well—we start this afternoon.

MOTHER. You want my daughter?

TALKER (*sadly*). Not your daughter, Madame.

MOTHER. What is it you want? Are you so backward in asking? It is not like the Master Johannes who came to my house eight days ago.

TALKER (*taking his courage in his hands*). Madame, though I have wandered about the world, I have saved some pennies in my time. A few trifling coins—enough for middle-age. Since I have had the great honour of knowing you—— (*He breaks off as the voice of the* SINGER *in full song is heard approaching.*) Oh, God

bless that poor young fool! Madame, I entreat
you——

MOTHER (*rising and moving hastily away*). Another time,
dear Johannes—(*she smiles very fondly at him as she goes
out*)—another time you must tell me—all.

>   (*The* TALKER *stares after her, hardly believing.*
>   *Then, with an air of solemn happiness, he takes*
>   *out his pipe and dances carefully but cheerfully*
>   *round the room, piping to himself. The* SINGER
>   *comes in singing merrily. He joins the* TALKER
>   *at the end of the room, turns round with him*
>   *and trips up and down the room with him, one*
>   *singing and the other piping.*)

TALKER. Friend, we are gay.

SINGER. Very, very gay, Master Johannes. (*They turn
round and go up and down the room as before.*)

TALKER. Something is stirring our middle-aged blood.
I feel years younger.

SINGER. I have only just been born.

TALKER (*with a wave of the hand*). Shall we take
another turn?

SINGER. At your pleasure. (*They go up and down as
before.*)

TALKER (*looking at the other anxiously out of the corners
of his eyes*). What do you think has happened to us?

SINGER (*with a similar look*). I—I wonder.

TALKER (*nervously*). I suppose the fact that we are
going off this afternoon—the joy of returning to our
old gay life is—is affecting us?

SINGER. I—I suppose so. (*Without enthusiasm*) Yes,
that must be it.

TALKER. This cauliflower existence, this settled life
which even the least enterprising cabbage would find
monotonous, we have had more than enough of it, my
friend.

SINGER. Yes. (*He sighs deeply.*) I sigh to think how we have wasted these eight days.

TALKER. Ah! (*He sighs still more deeply.*) However, Heaven be praised, we are for the road this afternoon.

SINGER (*gloomily*). Heaven be praised! It is a grand life.

TALKER (*carelessly*). Of course, if you came to me and said, " Johannes," you said, " I left my home in a fit of melancholy five months agone ; the melancholy is cured, I will return home again "—why, I would say, " God bless you, Master Duke ; go your way." Well, I can understand such a thing happening to a man of your age, not born to the wandering as I am.

SINGER. Bless you, Johannes, you are a true gentleman.

TALKER (*airily*). Say no more, say no more.

SINGER. But I cannot accept this sacrifice. I pledged myself to serve you for a year, and I'll keep my pledge.

TALKER (*considerably upset by this*). Wait a moment, Master Duke; I have myself thought of retiring these many months past. Indeed, it was only for your sake——

SINGER. No, no, I cannot allow it. It is only for my sake that you are saying this. We will take the road this afternoon. (*Heroically*) Indeed, I would infinitely prefer it. I am enamoured of the wandering life.

TALKER. It is a great life. It means everything to me.

> (*They stand side by side looking gloomily in front of them. Gradually they begin to glance towards each other ; they catch each other's eyes —and understand each other thoroughly.*)

TALKER (*clapping the* SINGER *heartily on the back*). I knew it, I knew it! You and the wandering life!

SINGER (*delightedly*). You, too, Johannes! You've had enough of it!

> (*They suddenly turn round and go up and down the room together, piping and singing. A genteel cough is heard outside the window, and the* MOTHER *is seen for a moment. The* TALKER *turns round with his pipe to his lips. They go up the room together again, and at the top the* TALKER, *with a wave of the hand, leaves his companion and goes out. He is seen passing the window.*)

The DAUGHTER *comes in.*

SINGER. Sweetheart!

DAUGHTER (*going to him*). Is it all right?

SINGER. Everything is all right, beloved.

DAUGHTER. You have told him?

SINGER (*nodding*). It couldn't have fallen out better. He, too, was tired of wandering and wanted to settle down.

DAUGHTER. I told mother. She seemed glad. You know, I think she seems younger about something.

Enter FIDDLER.

FIDDLER. Are we starting this afternoon?

DAUGHTER. Oh, Fiddler dear, do you mind very much? (*She holds out her hand, and the* SINGER *takes it.*) We aren't coming at all. We—we——

SINGER. We are getting married.

FIDDLER (*nodding to herself*). I thought so.

DAUGHTER. But you will come and stay with us sometimes. Oh, say you will!

SINGER (*smiling at* FIDDLER *with great friendliness*). Of course she will.

> (*The* TALKER *and the* MOTHER *are seen coming past the windows.*)

FIDDLER. There's Johannes. I expect we shall be starting this afternoon.

The TALKER and the MOTHER come in arm-in-arm. He bows to her and takes the floor.

TALKER. Ladies and gentlemen, companions-in-arms, knights and ladies of the road, comrades all,—I have the honour to make an announcement to you. The wandering company of the Red Feathers is determined from this date, likewise disbanded, or, as others would say, dissolved. "What means this, Master Johannes?" I hear you say. "Who has done this thing?" Ladies and gentles all, I answer you that young Cupid has done this thing. With unerring aim he has loosed his arrows. With the same happy arrow (*taking the* MOTHER's *hand*) he has pierced the hearts of this gracious lady and myself, while yonder gallant gentleman—I name no names, but the perspicacious will perceive whom I mean—is about to link his life with the charming maiden who stands so modestly by his side. There is one other noble lady present to whom I have not yet referred——

FIDDLER (*holding out her hand to the* MOTHER). I think I must go. Good-bye, and thank you.

MOTHER (*taking her hand and patting it*). Wait a moment, dear.

TALKER (*continuing his speech*)—noble lady to whom I have not yet referred. I will not hide from you the fact that she plays upon the fiddle with an elegance rarely to be heard. It is the earnest wish of (*swelling his chest*) my future wife and myself that she should take up her abode with us.

FIDDLER. It's very kind of you, but I don't think——

DAUGHTER (*coming across*). Mother, she's going to stay with *us ;* she promised.

MOTHER. It's sweet of you to ask her, dear, but I think it would be much more suitable that she should live with *us*.

SINGER. We should love to have her, and she could come and see you whenever she liked.

MOTHER. I was going to suggest that she should live with us and come and see *you* sometimes.

TALKER (*who has been thinking deeply*). I have it! What say you to this? For six months, making in all twenty-six weeks of the year, she shall live, reside, dwell, or, as one might say, take up her habitation with *us*; whereas for the other six months—— (*They have been so busy discussing the future of the* FIDDLER *that they have not noticed that she is no longer there. Suddenly the sound of the fiddle is heard.*) What's that?

The FIDDLER *comes in, wearing her cap now with the red feather in it. She is playing a wild song, a song of the road. She is content again. She goes up the room, and as she passes them she gives them a little bend of the head and the beginnings of a grave smile. She goes out of the door, still playing; she is still playing as she goes past the windows. They follow her with their eyes. When she is gone they still listen until the music dies in the distance.*

PRINTED IN GREAT BRITAIN BY
BILLING AND SONS, LTD., GUILDFORD AND ESHER

THE PHOENIX LIBRARY

Pocket size, 3s. 6d. net per volume.

8. BOOKS & CHARACTERS by LYTTON STRACHEY.

Studies, mainly of literary subjects. 'Mr. Strachey's is perhaps the finest critical intelligence at work in English literature to-day.' *The Times*.

9. FIERY PARTICLES by C. E. MONTAGUE.

'Nine of the best short stories in the language,' was the verdict of *The Sunday Express;* ' . . better than Kipling.'

10. FIRST PLAYS by A. A. MILNE.

Containing: 'Wurzel-Flummery,' 'The Lucky One,' 'The Boy Comes Home,' 'Belinda,' and 'The Red Feathers.'

11. CROME YELLOW by ALDOUS HUXLEY.

Mr. Huxley's first novel, perhaps his gayest. 'A delightful book.' *The Spectator*.

12. ART by CLIVE BELL.

In this book Mr. Clive Bell first propounded his theory of significant form. *Art* still remains the best short treatise in the English language on the æsthetics of visual art.

13. DISENCHANTMENT by C. E. MONTAGUE.

Mr. Montague's famous diagnosis of the moral results of the War. 'I have seen no book about the War so temperate and so human.' *John Masefield* in *The Manchester Guardian*.

14. THOSE BARREN LEAVES by ALDOUS HUXLEY.

A long novel. 'It is impossible to exhaust it at a first reading, and it should be kept and dipped into again and again.' *The Empire Review*.

15. VISION AND DESIGN by ROGER FRY.

Essays on art and artists by a master critic. Among the subjects are: 'Art and Life,' 'The Artist's Vision,' 'Negro Sculpture,' 'The French Post-Impressionists,' etc. 'It is a long time since we have come across a book so stimulating.' *The Daily Chronicle*.

16. ESSAYS OF A BIOLOGIST *by* JULIAN HUXLEY.

By the Professor of Zoology at King's College, the University of London. 'It is by a maker of new biological knowledge who is also a scholar and a poet.' *Prof. J. Arthur Thomson* in *The Observer*.

17. PLAYS *by* RICHARD HUGHES.

Previously issued by another publisher. Revised and reset. The contents are: 'The Sisters Tragedy,' 'A Comedy of Good and Evil' (of which *Mr. Bernard Shaw* wrote, 'Anyone who can't enjoy all this must be an idiot'), 'The Man Born to be Hanged' and 'Danger.'

18. LIMBO *by* ALDOUS HUXLEY.

Six stories ('Farcical History of Richard Greenow,' 'Happily Ever After,' 'Eupompus Gave Splendour to Art by Numbers,' 'Cynthia,' 'The Bookshop,' and 'The Death of Lully') and a one-act play, 'Happy Families.'

19. SECOND PLAYS *by* A. A. MILNE.

Containing: 'Mr. Pim Passes By'; 'The Romantic Age'; 'Make Believe'; 'The Camberley Triangle' and 'The Stepmother.'

20. THE RIGHT PLACE *by* C. E. MONTAGUE.

A book on holiday travel, of which *The Sunday Times* said: 'A tonic to the mind and spirit of man, his book cannot be overpraised.'

21. THE SAILOR'S RETURN *by* DAVID GARNETT.

Mr. Garnett's third story, longer than either *Lady Into Fox* or *A Man in the Zoo*, one which was hailed by *The Empire Review* as 'a masterpiece.'

22. MORTAL COILS *by* ALDOUS HUXLEY.

Short stories, containing 'The Gioconda Smile,' 'Permutations among the Nightingales,' 'The Tillotson Banquet,' 'Green Tunnels,' and 'Nuns at Luncheon.'

23. MR. WESTON'S GOOD WINE *by* T. F. POWYS.

The first unlimited edition of Mr. Powys's longest and greatest story. 'Worthy at once to take its place among the great allegories of English literature.' *The Bookman*.

32. SWANN'S WAY, vol. 1, *by* MARCEL PROUST.

Translated by C. K. SCOTT MONCRIEFF. 'M. Proust is a genius; and Mr. Scott Moncrieff has treated him like one.' *The Nation.*

33. SWANN'S WAY, vol. 2, *by* MARCEL PROUST.

Translated by C. K. SCOTT MONCRIEFF. 'The translator . . . faced a task of prodigious difficulty with extraordinary success.' *The London Mercury.*

34. ESSAYS IN POPULAR SCIENCE by JULIAN HUXLEY.

'One of the few scientific books that is popular and scientific without patronising the reader.' *Cambridge Review.*

35. A SHORT HISTORY OF ENGLAND
by G. K. CHESTERTON.

'He is at once the most concise and fullest historian this country has yet found.' *The Observer.*

36. TWO OR THREE GRACES *by* ALDOUS HUXLEY.

Four stories, one as long as a short novel. 'I have no hesitation in saying that of the younger men writing to-day, Mr. Huxley is in a class by himself.' *Ralph Straus* in *The Bystander.*

37. HADRIAN VII *by* FR. ROLFE ('Baron Corvo.')

A novel. 'There is no precedent for it in English literature.' *A. J. A. Symons* in *Life and Letters.*

38. THE GENTLE ART OF COOKERY
by MRS. C. F. LEYEL *and* MISS OLGA HARTLEY.

A really original cookery book which 'no properly instituted home should be without.' *The Morning Post.*

39. ROUGH JUSTICE *by* C. E. MONTAGUE.

A novel. 'A beautiful and a terrible book. . . . A masterpiece of fiction.' *Sir Philip Gibbs* in *The Catholic Times.*

40. FOUR PLAYS *by* A. A. MILNE.

Containing: 'To Have the Honour'; 'Ariadne, or Business First'; 'Portrait of a Gentleman in Slippers'; and 'Success.'

41. SINCE CÉZANNE *by* Clive Bell.
   'All who have ever asked the question, "What is Art?" should read this collection of essays.' *The Manchester Guardian.*

42. IN THE BEGINNING *by* Norman Douglas.
   A romance. 'The nearest approach in our language to the manner of Anatole France.' *The Spectator.*

43. WITHIN A BUDDING GROVE, vol. 1
   by Marcel Proust.
   'That unapproachable triumph of the translator, mr. scott moncrieff's translation of Proust's *A l'Ombre des Jeunes Filles en Fleurs.' The New Statesman.*

44. WITHIN A BUDDING GROVE, vol. 2
   by Marcel Proust.
   'mr. scott moncrieff's translation continues as well as it began.' *The Observer.*

45. PROPER STUDIES *by* Aldous Huxley.
   Essays. 'Brilliantly illuminating.' *Arnold Bennett* in *The Evening Standard.*

46. MR. TASKER'S GODS *by* T. F. Powys.
   A story. 'A little epic of the divine at war with the human.' *The Outlook.*

47. DON TARQUINIO *by* Fr. Rolfe ('Baron Corvo.')
   A romance. 'It has the irresponsible high spirits of the youth of the world.' *The Daily Mail.*

48. TWENTIETH CENTURY POETRY
   an anthology by Harold Monro.
   'The best anthology of the moderns that I have seen.' *The Evening Standard.* Also available in leather, 5s.

49. JESTING PILATE *by* Aldous Huxley.
   The diary of a journey. 'It must be a sedative type of reader who lays down this volume without having been stimulated, amused, and probably annoyed.' *Sir Edmund Gosse* in *The Sunday Times.*

50. DUSTY ANSWER *by* Rosamond Lehmann.
   'A. N.' Said in *The Sunday Times* of *Dusty Answer*: 'It is not often that one can say with confidence of a first novel that it reveals new possibilities for literature.'

61. FABLES *by* T. F. Powys.

The first unlimited edition of a book which *The Sunday Times* rightly called 'a work of art.'

62. THE GUERMANTES WAY, vol. 1
by Marcel Proust.

Translated by C. K. Scott Moncrieff. 'Where mortal can extract the essence, this translator has done so.' *The Times Literary Supplement.*

63. THE GUERMANTES WAY, vol. 2
by Marcel Proust.

Translated by C. K. Scott Moncrieff 'into distinguished English.' *The Times Literary Supplement.*

Spring, 1931:

64. BRIEF CANDLES *by* Aldous Huxley.

Containing 'Chawdron,' 'The Rest Cure,' 'The Claxtons,' and 'After the Fireworks.'

65. THE CHARTERHOUSE OF PARMA *by* Stendhal.

C. K. Scott Moncrieff's magnificent translation, in one volume of 720 pages.

66. HOW ABOUT EUROPE? *by* Norman Douglas.

'It compels you to think. . . . It compels you to laugh.' *Arnold Bennett* in *The Evening Standard.*

67. SELECTED POEMS OF COVENTRY PATMORE.

Edited with a preface by his grandson, Derek Patmore.

68. THE JOURNAL OF A DISAPPOINTED MAN
by W. N. P. Barbellion.

Now recognized as one of the most enduring books of the century. 'Will be devoured by thousands.' *The Nation.*

69. AN ANTHOLOGY OF 18th CENTURY POETRY
by W. J. Turner.

A collection made by a distinguished modern poet.

CHATTO & WINDUS
97 & 99 St. Martin's Lane, W.C. 2